Norf(

Memories of a
Ba
Wells-next-the-Sea

Recorded by Brian Barker
Editing and additional text by David Lowe

© *Copyright 2003 Brian Barker and David Lowe*
The moral rights of the authors are asserted under the Copyright, Designs and Patents Act 1988.

Published by David Lowe www.davidlowe.org
ISBN: 0-9542534-1-8

Printed in Great Britain by Norfolk Central Printers, Wells-next-the-Sea, Norfolk

All rights reserved. No part of this publication may be reprinted or reproduced or utilised in any form or by any electronic, mechanical or other means, now known or hereinafter invented, including photocopying and recording, or in any information, storage or retrieval system without permission in writing from the publisher.

DEDICATION

This account of my working life is dedicated to the many people who helped me throughout the years; especially to my father Leslie and grandfather Herbert Barker who between them had the foresight to start a carrier business in Wells, and to my mother Marjorie who always encouraged me, particularly during the difficult times.

Special thanks are due to my wife Madge and our sons Christopher and Philip for their continuing support; they must have thought that this memoir would never be completed.

Brian Barker

Acknowledgement

The authors wish to acknowledge the help of family and friends in reading and commenting upon the draft manuscripts for this book, without which it might have contained many errors. Thanks are also due to Timothy Doyle who prepared the pictures for printing – some of them very old and faded.

Leslie and Marjorie Barker with the Ford Model 'T' taxi which was used to start the Barker business in the 1920s.

The Authors

This book is as much the story of Brian Barker's life in the local carrier and road haulage business founded by his father and grandfather as it is about the business itself. His story unfolds in the text as he recounts his many memories of fifty years as a Norfolk carrier, road haulier and warehouseman, shipping agent and garage proprietor in Wells-next-the Sea. Even now, in his seventies, the same flush of enthusiasm that must have inspired his early entry into the carrying business still shines through as his prodigious memory takes him, and us, back through the troubles and strife, the high days and heydays of a long and varied transport career. The *Eastern Daily Press* headlined its 29 September 2000 news item on the final closure of the family business: 'End of road for the great survivors'. Brian must be a survivor, besides sustaining the family business to the bitter end as this story recounts, he has supported Norwich City football team – the Canaries – through thick and thin, like his father before him, since boyhood.

For his part, Brian says:
> *"I am very proud and privileged to have been part of this successful family business. Its story is something I originally wanted to record purely for my own family, but the Wells Local History Society invited me to record a piece for the town's history and then David Lowe came along and suggested that other people might also be interested to learn how a small family business had survived so many ups and downs over the generations; hence this book."*

Co-author David Lowe is also Norfolk born with road haulage in his blood. Following in the footsteps of his father, who worked for the old Carter Paterson (PX) parcels company in Surrey Street, Norwich, he started his transport career in general haulage as a trainee with British Road Services (BRS) in Norwich during the de-nationalisation years between 1952 and 1954. His earliest memorable connection with Wells-next-the-Sea was in 1953 while working in a temporary BRS office on the quayside helping to organise the onward movement of imported rock gypsum destined for fertiliser production.

After many years in road haulage and distribution management, David turned to transport journalism and has spent the past thirty-five years writing about the industry, becoming a well-known, award-winning, author of many best-selling transport law and management manuals. He is a Fellow of the Chartered Institute of Logistics and Transport, a Freeman of the City of London and a Liveryman of the esteemed and historic Worshipful Company of Carmen.

In 1997 David returned to his Norfolk roots after living abroad for a number of years. He regularly visits the North Norfolk coast to absorb the magic of its winter bleakness and the sound of screaming seagulls scavenging in Wells harbour.

Preface

This is the story of a Norfolk family business of general carriers, which later turned to road haulage, warehousing and shipping. It was founded in the years just after the end of the First World War when vehicles were a far cry from the sophisticated hi-tech trucks we see today and the roads, even the main routes, were significantly inferior to the very worst we currently have to endure. The good years for the firm were from the 1940s to the 1980s, the demise setting in from the time when road haulage licensing deregulation started letting all and sundry into the industry, when trades unions put undue pressure on employers and when fuel prices and vehicle road tax rates went through the roof, bringing the business to final closure in the first year of the new millennium.

The local general motor carrier was a familiar sight on our roads for half a century or more, until replaced from the 1970s by the proliferation of road haulage firms springing up under the deregulated licensing system and proclaiming such service mottos as 'Express Parcels' and 'Next Day Delivery' as though this was some revolutionary new concept. Some firms even pretentiously called themselves 'global logistics providers', although few in those early days could legitimately claim to provide such far-reaching services.

These local or general carriers, as they were variously called, were predominantly small local firms. Invariably, they had just one or two lorries used for carrying 'smalls' or parcels traffic, although not all consignments were of conventional 'parcel' shape or dimensions – far from it. In fact, they comprised every sort, shape and size of goods imaginable; packed and wrapped, or not, as the case may be. Broadly, carriers worked on the principle that, if something could be lifted up by one or two men, it could be carried in a lorry, bearing in mind that there was very little in the way of lifting equipment available in those early days. These carriers served their local communities, picking up and carrying almost anything that individuals, local shops and businesses needed transporting; as will be seen as this fascinating story unfolds.

They were largely restricted by the terms of the licensing conditions that controlled their activities from 1933 until deregulation of the old system of carrier licensing in 1970. Nevertheless, they invariably provided good service and regularly collected and delivered orders on the same day or, without fail, the next day – this was the service that customers expected.

While there were a few reliable nationwide delivery networks and a limited amount of overnight trunking between depots or centres prior to the 1950s, the concept of centralised sorting 'hubs' and 'hub-and-spoke' delivery networks was still very much in its infancy and they were nothing like the sophisticated operations that we see today. And, of course, in those days such technologies as computerised route planning and scheduling of deliveries, electronic consignment tracking, mobile telephone networks and global positioning satellites (gps) were all yet to be thought of and developed into the 'hi-tech' systems that ensure the efficiency of today's express parcels delivery industry.

Despite the shortcomings of the age, most local carriers ran strictly controlled and efficient operations - in so far as road conditions, the weather and the foibles of early motor vehicles would allow. And these operations were carried out with as much concern for cost control and profitability as their modern-day counterparts. They had to be run as tight ships. Customers, as always, held the whip hand, being free to chose another firm if their regular carrier failed to meet service expectations.

Footnote:
The Norfolk town of East Dereham, which features in this story, formally changed its name to Dereham in 1991.

Origins and Early Years

Barker and Sons of Wells-next-the-Sea in North Norfolk, like so many small general carrying firms throughout the country, provided what in their day were first-class carrying services for traders, shopkeepers and local inhabitants across their region; in Barker's case, principally between North and West Norfolk and the main centres of Norwich and King's Lynn.

From shortly after the end of the First World War, when motor lorries largely replaced horse-drawn transport, right up to the late 1960s, when the business changed to long distance haulage, the firm provided a local general collection and delivery service for most types of goods that people needed moving from one place to another. At a time when very few businesses had their own delivery vans and even fewer households had access to a motor vehicle to move their possessions, the general carrier was relied upon for fetching and carrying all the goods and chattels that shopkeepers, small manufacturing businesses, or even private individuals, could not collect and carry themselves either on foot or in a bus or taxi.

Typically, in Barkers' case, the items collected and delivered ranged through fresh fruit and vegetables, bread, groceries, beer, furniture and household utensils, coal, bicycles, tools, motor parts, farming and agricultural supplies, vehicle tyres, boots and shoes and a myriad of other consignments both small and large, most falling into the category that we now define as consumer goods. Usually the collection point was a main wholesaler, repairer or manufacturer; for Barkers, many of these were in Norwich or in the market towns of King's Lynn, Fakenham, Swaffham, East Dereham and Cromer, while the deliveries covered the coastal resorts, villages, farms and industrial premises across the whole of North and North West Norfolk.

Before the Great War of 1914-1918 most cartage was by horse-drawn wagon and many of today's well-known road haulage firms can trace their beginnings to these days. Names such as Pickfords, whose ancestry indicates that one Thomas Pickford provided packhorse services as far back as 1646; the Shore Porters Society of Aberdeen, founded in 1498 and still in business today; and Carter Paterson, founded in 1860, subsumed into the state-owned haulage operations of BRS Parcels in the 1950s and subsequently into the present-day Lynx Express Parcels. These are just a few of the many household names synonymous with the history of road haulage in Great Britain.

The old railway companies, long before they were nationalised to form British Rail, long, even, before the First World War, also delivered parcels by road with horse-drawn wagons, and so did many of the local co-operative societies. But a large proportion of local carrier businesses were founded following the war-end in 1918 when many young soldiers returning from France, and thankful for being spared the fate of many of their comrades, were seeking new challenges. A surfeit of unwanted and discarded military lorries provided just the opportunity for these men who had first learned to drive and maintain these vehicles among the poppy fields of Flanders and the mud of Ypres on the Western Front.

Most of these small carrier businesses thrived until deregulation of the road haulage industry in 1970 when the old A, B and C carriers' licensing system, based on proof of need, was abolished to be replaced by a new 'Operator' (O) licensing system which allowed virtually anybody to start running haulage vehicles, provided only that they could meet certain meagre standards of quality and safety. Thus the trade protection offered by the old so-called 'quantity' licensing system was lost in this new era of open competition, driven solely by market forces, which largely spelled the death-knell for the licensed local independent carrier and an era of road transport history faded into oblivion. All this, of course, was before the widespread adoption of palletised freight, before the growth of the express parcels transport sector as we currently know it, and before the arrival of refrigerated food lorries, hydraulic tail-lifts and the many other specially-equipped vehicles that we see delivering in the High Street today.

The Early Days

Father and son Herbert and Leslie Barker founded their general motor carrier business in 1928, having, from 1921, run a successful taxi business at the small coastal town of Wells-next-the-Sea on the North Norfolk coast. Herbert Barker was born in 1872 in the Barsham area. He went to London to become a tailor and later returned to North Norfolk to run the *Three Horseshoes* Warham, a public house that has changed very little over the years and looks very much today as it would have done in the days when Herbert was the landlord. It has few concessions to modern day life – a notice on the bar says No chips and No credit cards. Herbert died in 1938. His son Leslie Sizeland Barker was born in London in 1900, but returned with his father to live at the pub in Warham before joining the Royal Flying Corps during the First World War. Leslie's son Brian, the third Barker generation in the business, has early memories of his father running the general carrier business between Wells and Norwich and recounts here how he carried it on until the late 1960s before changing over to long-distance haulage in 1970, later adding warehousing and shipping activities when brother Graham joined the business.

The family Bible, in which the first entry is 1870, shows that Leslie Barker's family originated from the Mileham and Barsham areas of North West Norfolk. Family friend Alan Dunsdon, who researched the Barker side of the family, found that Brian's great-great-grandfather Barker was a guilder and frame maker in Fakenham. Leslie married Marjorie Yarham, whose family, the Yarhams and the Spooners were from Wighton and Wells-next-the-Sea in North Norfolk. Brian remembers that Grandfather Yarham at one time had a coal business on Wells quay that was eventually carried on by his son Sydney until around 1970. Marjorie Barker ran the Ostrich Guest House in Wells throughout the Second World War, mainly for Air Sea Rescue crews based in the town, and for many years afterwards. She also took over Mr Sherwood's shoe shop in the High Street.

Grandfather Yarham,(in bowler hat) with his coal lorry outside the old Maltings on the Quay at Wells, around 1930

Bracing Wells
Wells is best known today for its bracing air and its shellfish. Indeed, so bracing is it that standing on the town quay on a winter's day, with the freezing wind from the north penetrating your bones, it is not difficult to appreciate that, apart from a stretch of low-lying salt marsh just beyond the harbour and a few oil and gas platforms far out in the North Sea, there is nothing between you and the North Pole to interrupt its passage. And this was one of the principal shortcomings to be overcome by the fledgling Barker business; their trade could come only from three sides, an approximate semi-circle from the North Norfolk coast down as far as Norwich in the south. It was not until many years later that they were able to benefit from the trade that came in from the sea.

Young Leslie Barker must have stood at Wells railway station many times, waiting for arriving train passengers to use his taxi service to take them the short journey down to the beach. He might have reflected too, if he had the time and the inclination to stop on the town quay on his way back to the station, that for over 1100 years men had stood there looking out to sea for approaching vessels. Originally they might have feared marauding invaders from the north, but in much later times, trading ships brought in essential supplies. In Leslie's early days it was the holidaymakers with their luggage and buckets and spades who provided the welcome influx of trade. But the holidaymakers were not the only arrivals by rail; in winter Leslie must have stood at the station many a time, probably frozen and braced against the arctic winds that percolated through the town, while he awaited the wealthy parties who came up from London in their tweeds to take part in Lord Leicester's shooting weekends at nearby Holkham Hall – more good business for the Barker taxi service.

The modern town of Wells-next-the-Sea has a long trading history. Formerly it was known as Quella and is recorded as such in the Domesday Book, then being just a small inlet on the North Norfolk coast settled by invading Danes in about 865AD. But by the eighteenth century it had become a prosperous trading port, busy with malt exports and Icelandic codfish being regularly shipped to London. On the return, ships brought in salt for fish packing, sugar and coal - even shipments of brandy were recorded. A century later the port's exports were mainly grain and oysters while coal, timber and linseed were its principal imports.

In the middle of the nineteenth century the railway came to Wells, serving the town and port until the station finally closed in 1964. It was the railway that put the town into the history books when, in 1879, a passenger train overran the buffers, crashed through the station wall, demolishing the toilets in the process, and killed a local coachman. Not that this was the town's first claim to notoriety; it was also said to be the birthplace, in 1752, of one John Fryer who, in due course, became sailing master on the *Bounty* under Captain Bligh.

Today, Wells is a fishing haven renowned for its oysters, crabs, lobsters, cockles and mussels, and as a growing beach resort. The railway is long gone, the big ships can no longer sail into the silted-up port and part of the harbour office has become a maritime museum. The once-busy quay is a now a public car park faced by a row of amusement arcades, souvenir shops and a plethora of cafes and fish and chip shops. The old, once busy, granaries and maltings are now used for other purposes. The last ship of any size to enter the port was in 2001 when the 100-foot Dutch sailing barge *Albatros*, that used to arrive regularly from Holland loaded with Soya for Dalgety at Egmere, near North Creake, berthed here for the last time, remaining as a permanent home for its charismatic Dutch owner-skipper, Ton Brouwer. And, under pressure of present day economics, the year of the new millennium saw the final demise of the locally based carrier business that Herbert and Leslie Barker started all those years ago.

Getting Started

It was the railway that got Leslie Barker started in business. Following his demobilisation from the Royal Flying Corps in 1918, at the end of the First World War, his mechanical skills, learned as an aircraft fitter, were a good grounding for joining forces with his father Herbert to start the family taxi business. Between times they also ran a timber business, buying up felled trees on the Holkham estate and selling the cut-up logs as firewood around the town and local villages.

As their ambitions expanded, father and son exchanged the taxi for a Ford model 'T' open truck and started running goods to London two or three times weekly. Ever on the look out for more trade, they quickly secured a contract to collect Sunlight Soap from Hays Wharf in London for delivery on the way back to Wells. Not content solely with the revenues from the carrier business, the Barkers also looked for other opportunities, among which was a worthwhile contract secured with local magnate Mr Kitson. He owned a number of properties in London, where the Barkers were engaged to take him regularly to collect his rents. What is quite amazing, by today's standards, is that they travelled all the way back to Wells carrying hundreds of pounds in cash despite what, even then, would have been the quite considerable risk of robbery en-route. On one occasion, in the quest for revenue-earning loads, they even carried a corpse from Wells for burial in London; a job that became the talk of the firm for years to come, and no wonder! In those days of poor roads and very few streetlights, the route took them through a very dark Epping Forest with its overhanging trees, which the crew found very spooky indeed knowing what was riding just behind them in the back of the lorry!

From around 1928 Leslie Barker was running the business as a general carrier, operating mainly between Wells and Norwich. By the time the Second World War started in 1939 the business had expanded to two vehicles. The old Ford had been replaced by a Bedford truck and then later supplemented by the addition of a single-rear-wheel type Chevrolet, built in those days by Bedford [owned by Vauxhall Motors] at Luton. Brian describes how this vehicle, his father's pride and joy, won a competition for the 'Best-kept vehicle in Norfolk' organised by Delves of Norwich in 1930 [co-incidentally, the year of Brian's arrival on the scene], in those days the local Bedford and Chevrolet truck distributor. Brian still has the winner's silver cigarette case presented to his father at the time, and it still contains the cigarettes that were part of the prize – albeit now a little aged and disintegrated.

The pre-war success of Leslie's business was, unfortunately, to be short-lived due to the many restrictions imposed as the country geared up for another war (WWII). In fact, the fleet was quickly reduced to half its size when the Chevrolet was commandeered for war service and converted to become the local Air Raid Post (ARP) ambulance for the town. The remaining Bedford truck, driven by employee driver Fred Raisborough, whose job was classified as a 'reserved occupation', continued on the parcels-carrying operations right throughout the war. The loads were mainly of food and clothing, essential supplies to shops and commodities for the government. The Barker lorry, along with those of other government sub-contractors, would collect loads of much-needed items for delivery to local NAAFI canteens, aerodromes and other military locations in North and West Norfolk.

The Carrier Years

There was good news for Leslie Barker in 1945 when the compulsorily requisitioned Chevrolet lorry was returned to the firm after its war service. At about the same time the third generation of Barkers joined the business. Brian, son of Leslie and grandson of Herbert, was born in March 1930 at the Old Coastguard Houses, off Freeman Street in Wells. By the time he was 15 years old he had left Thetford Grammar School and started full-time work as a van boy learning the ropes, although he had spent many hours on the vans before this, taking every opportunity during his school holidays to get out on the road.

Practising for a career in road haulage. Three-year old Brian gets a feel for four-wheeled transport.

His first recollections as a young child in the early 1930s were of his father taking him up the Warham Road to see the Flying Circus that had come to the town. He remembers both the old Chevrolet lorry and the Bedford used in the carrying business. He also recalls, even to this day, one particular occasion when his father and grandfather took him out with the lorry on the delivery rounds. While crossing a ford between the Walsingham villages, they stopped right in the middle of the deep water. Standing the very young Brian on the lorry running board, they jokingly made out that the vehicle had broken down and said that he would have to jump down into the water and go to get help!

On another occasion, when he was about 10 or 11 years old, Brian remembers being in the lorry coming up the hill at Stiffkey on a winter's day heading home along the North Norfolk coastal road from Blakeney.

"Unfortunately, the vehicle got stuck halfway up the hill in the freezing conditions and despite all his efforts Father could just not get it going again, instead it started to slide back down the hill. I jumped out and because it was so slippery I was able to push the lorry into the bank to stop it sliding further. We were then able to find some earth to spread under the rear wheels to get it going again and reach the top of the hill.

During the Second World War one of my father's lorries, a Chevrolet single-rear-wheel model built in those days by Bedford at Luton, was taken over by the Government and converted to become the local Air Raid Post ambulance. It was garaged behind the Crown Hotel in the town and I remember seeing it there. After the war during which Father carried on with the Bedford lorry, he got the Chevrolet back and we re-started the deliveries round the coast. I was about 15 years old then."

It was during the war years that Brian gained much of his early experience on the lorry and had one of his most frightening experiences. At school holiday time, he acted as van boy for his father's employee driver, Fred Raisborough. Fred had worked for Leslie Barker for a number of years, latterly as a driver on the general carrying business, but in former times working also for Leslie's wood business. In those days, Fred would go into Holkham Park and pick up treetops that the foresters had cut out and, sometimes with Brian's help, would saw-up the wood, cart it back to Wells where they chopped it into logs for firewood and then sold it round the villages.

Fred's main job, however, was to drive the delivery lorry doing the parcels collections and deliveries on the Wells to Norwich run, and whenever Brian got the opportunity he went with him as the van boy. He recalls:

"I remember on one occasion during the war, we were coming along St Benedict's Street, Norwich towards the Dereham Road, and just crossing Barn Road, heading out of the City, when we heard the air-raid sirens; first the warning and then the crash alarm. Somebody came out into the road and put up their hands to stop us and turn us into Orchard Street where there were air-raid shelters built on the street. These shelters had a single entrance in the middle and I ran in to one side and Fred went to the other. The side I went in was full of ladies who wanted to know where I came from, but in the middle of this chat there was an almighty explosion as a bomb hit just a few streets away. It was my first experience of the war and it was very frightening."

After these enlightening experiences, when he left school Brian was given his head to carry on the business and began to expand the coverage. Meanwhile, the firm had acquired two brand-spanking new Austin 3-tonners when such vehicles first became available after the war. These came from local distributor Massey & Bridges of Fakenham. They were fitted with flatbed bodies, for which Mr Huggins, the blacksmith at the North Norfolk village of North Creake, made hoop-frames over which the tarpaulin covers protecting the loads were fixed. The work was divided up, one lorry doing the Norwich collections and deliveries and the other doing the collections and deliveries around the North Norfolk villages. The firm also expanded its territory, delivering as far out as the Hunstanton area to the west and taking in Holt and the Cromer area to the north and east. The route from Fakenham to Norwich was extended on one or two days a week to take in East Dereham on one side of the main A1067 Norwich to Fakenham road and Foulsham and Reepham on the other side.

One of the Barker lorries delivering in Holt town centre (1950s)
Courtesy EDPpics

Brian's job as a 15-year-old van boy was to help loading and unloading the parcels, acting as 'mate' for the driver, but it also entailed becoming familiar with the loads, the journeys and the requirements of customers. And, of course, he never failed to grab every possible chance that arose to get behind the wheel for a little 'under-age' driving. He had been learning the basics of driving from the age of 11 or 12 years and had actually been driving the lorries from about age 13, instructed by Fred Raisborough, and practising in places that were safe, such as on farms and airfields. He passed his driving test as soon as he reached the official age of 17 years in 1947, and started driving the lorry on parcels deliveries from that very first day. As he recalls,

"I went to King's Lynn for my driving test. It was the day of our normal Hunstanton round so Dad said to Mother that he would take the car and she could sit with me in the lorry (she had a full driving licence but didn't drive in those days) to Docking where we would leave it while we went into King's Lynn for my test in the car, hoping that I would pass and could get on with delivering the round. Well, sure enough I did pass (Mother says she saw me going round in King's Lynn with the examiner and she said she knew I would pass by the look of determination on my face!). So we came back to Docking and I went off to work straight away with the lorry delivering the Hunstanton round."

Shortly after this, like most young men at the time, Brian was called up for two years' compulsory National Service with the RAF, which he spent not so far from home, being based conveniently at RAF Coltishall in Norfolk. Returning to Civvy Street in 1950, Brian took up the reins again, but now with the elevated task of actually running the family carrier business himself with its two lorries, father Leslie having decided to retire from lorry driving.

During this immediate post-war period the firm was very busy, so much so that father Leslie, despite being supposedly retired, was doing local deliveries (surreptitiously, because it was illegal under the carrier licensing rules) with the little Morris Eight family car with a trailer hitched up to the tow-bar to free up the lorries so they could continue with the Norwich collections and deliveries.

Brian at the wheel of one of the Austin parcels vehicles shortly after passing his driving test

Under Brian's management the business prospered throughout the 1950s and 1960s. As the years progressed the original lorries had worn out, but the firm did not have the money to replace them with new models at that time so they looked around for second-hand vehicles. Brian says he remembers once going all the way to Edgware Road, London to buy a Ford that had a tall box-type body but when he got it back to Wells it was found to be too tall for their City rounds so they had to cut it down.

Regular trade was building up across quite a large territory extending from Wisbech right across to Norwich then northwards to Holt and Cromer and back along the coast to King's Lynn. Daily services between Wells and Norwich continued, with some forty collections every day from the Norwich wholesalers for deliveries to the main towns in North Norfolk such as East Dereham, Fakenham and Burnham Market, and to the villages of North and South Creake, all of which constituted the firm's basic rounds. Once the firm had obtained its third carrier licence, new daily services were added to the key market towns of King's Lynn and Wisbech.

Nevertheless, the firm was still hampered by having its back to the sea, so all revenues had to be earned from within that somewhat limited semi-circular territory. But despite not having exclusivity of the parcels trade in their area, since there were a number of keen competitors, trade was nevertheless buoyant and the Barker fleet quickly grew to four lorries.

The Licensing Restrictions
Unlike today's, post-1970, de-regulated haulage scene, where a haulier can add as many vehicles as he wishes to his fleet provided he can show he has suitable maintenance facilities and adequate financial resources to operate them safely, in the days of carrier licensing restriction under the Road and Rail Traffic Act 1933, an operator had to prove there was a definite need for extended operations or additional vehicles if he wished to expand his business. This was difficult with both local competitors and the railways always ready to raise objection on the grounds that they already had sufficient spare capacity to handle any loads offered by customers. Applicants for licence variation needed to produce supporting letters and evidence from potential customers to the Traffic Commissioner justifying the need for extra capacity. Sometimes even an appearance by the customer in person before the Traffic Commissioner at a Public Inquiry was necessary. Invariably this proved to be a gruelling ordeal for the operator following tortuous face-to-face confrontations before a Road-Rail Negotiating Committee at which arch trading enemies could effectively shoot down the applicant's claims.

From the time of transport nationalisation in 1947, special dispensation was required to operate beyond 25 miles from base. The firm's two open 'A' carriers' licences, which Leslie Barker had held since the beginnings of carrier licensing in 1933, were likewise restricted to this 25 mile limit, but to deliver into Norwich required authorisation to cover a 32-mile radius. However, with the support of local Member of Parliament Mr Gooch, the licences were extended to enable the important Norwich operation to continue.

Unfailing Regularity

We shall see the continuing effects of licensing restrictions on the Barker business as this story unfolds. However, even with its A licences restricted the business remained extremely busy in the early 1950s with Brian at the helm. With his retentive memory he can vividly recount the customers, the routes and the collection and delivery locations they served over many years. Much of the work was, of course, carried out with unfailing regularity, but every now and then some highlight or humorous escapade would enlighten a long and humdrum day. And the firm was not alone in this trade in those days; it had a number of keen competitors such as English Brothers of Fakenham, Munroes at North Walsham, Mr Heseltine from Cley and Moores of Sheringham. They, like Barkers, all had depots in Norwich although the term 'depot' was perhaps a grandiose description for what were no more than their own 'sheds', located in public house yards. Barkers' depot was at the Coach and Horses Inn on Orford Place in Norwich while English Brothers had their depot in Bethel Street and some of the other firms used the Lamb Inn at the Back of the Inns in the City.

People who had goods to be taken back to North Norfolk would bring their parcels to these sheds and leave them for Barkers (or one of the other firms) to pick up – nobody used to worry about signatures in those days, Brian recalls. Sometimes these parcels would be from private individuals, but some of the local wholesalers would also leave small consignments for delivery, although Barkers did a regular run around the main Norwich wholesalers collecting from their premises. These parcels would be delivered and the carriage charges collected from the consignee on a 'carriage forward', or a 'cash-on-delivery' basis if necessary.

Reliability was one of the keystones to the great success of the Barker business. For example, Brian clearly remembers one particular job they did regularly for many years. First thing every

Monday morning, when leaving the Wells garage in Freeman Street, they had to call at the Co-operative shop, also in Freeman Street, where the manager was Mr James and his assistant was Miss Butcher, to pick up the shop's accounts books and take them to the main Co-op shop in Fakenham for checking and then collect them up the next day to bring back to Wells. The day's work invariably started at 7 am and the first job would be to unload the goods that had arrived on the lorry from Norwich the previous evening. These would be sorted into their different delivery areas, as far as Burnham Market to the west and Blakeney and Binham to the east of Wells.

Happy Recollections
Brian's prodigious memory works overtime when reflecting on his 'carrier' days of the 1940s and 1950s. He recalls many enjoyable jobs undertaken and humorous incidents that occurred during these early days on the lorries. One of the jobs he says he most enjoyed was when they delivered supplies to local aerodromes and army bases on a sub-contract basis for the government. They used to get a telephone message to call at the Hall Road depot in Norwich of Eastern Roadways, a prominent East Anglian road haulage firm [coincidentally, the same depot where some years later co-author David Lowe started his career in road haulage when Eastern Roadways had become part of the state-owned British Road Services]. The order would be to collect a variety of goods for delivery to these military locations in North Norfolk – mainly 56 lb boxes of butter, sugar and barrels of beer, but, to Brian's dismay, nothing exciting like guns and bullets.

Delivering beer in barrels was another Barker speciality, a job they used to do for Cawdrons of Fakenham and Wells who bottled it for sale under their own label. The particular interest here was the fact that these barrels held either 18 or 36 gallons, the latter being about as much as a man could handle, and they were certainly very difficult to manoeuvre. Cawdrons used to supply a 'skid' that hooked on the back of the lorry so the barrels could be slid down easily and safely. Yet another outsized and difficult-to-handle load that Brian remembers encountering on a regular basis was the collection and delivery of large-size tractor wheels and tyres for farms. Generally, they were carried to and from the main tyre suppliers and repairers in Norwich to the local tyre distributors in the North Norfolk area, both Baxters and Southgates of Fakenham being prime examples of firms who held permits to supply tyres during the war. Of course, in those days there were no fully equipped roadside tyre-service vans of the type we see on the road today for on-site repairs, neither did farms have suitable equipment for removing tyres from wheels. Thus, if a tractor tyre was punctured or damaged, the whole wheel and tyre assembly had to be removed and taken complete into Norwich for repair.

Brian remembers one particular occasion when for the first time he and driver Fred had two of these large tractor tyres for delivery to Baxters.

"We had stood them up inside the lorry, strapped to the side and when it came to unloading them because they were so heavy we just pushed them off the tailboard, not thinking that once they had dropped the four feet to the ground they would bounce six feet into the air ... and then keep on bouncing. The first one we pushed off bounced once, twice, and then three times and headed straight on...right through the wall of Baxters' wooden parts store!"

In those early days there was neither the need for, nor much concern about, vehicle and load security – unlike today when lorry crime is rife, with millions of pounds worth of goods being stolen annually. He remembers, for example, going in the lorry with his father, a keen football fan, an enthusiasm that rubbed off on Brian, to see Norwich City play at Carrow Road on an occasion when the famous star of the day, Tommy Lawton, was in the war-time side.

"Anyway, that morning we got a telephone call to pick up a load of cigarettes from Churchman's depot in Prince of Wales Road, Norwich, not far from the Carrow Road football ground, so we collected this load before going on to the match and would you believe, when we got there the cigarettes, loaded in wooden cases, were standing,

unguarded, out on the pavement! We loaded them then left them in the unguarded lorry while we watched the match! You couldn't do that today!"

Not only tractor tyres, but also many other types of vehicle tyres and motor components formed much of Barkers' Norwich business after the war. They collected new tyres for the local garages and shops from the Johnson Burton & Theobald [commonly called JBTs] depot in St Peter's Street, Norwich [this street, opposite the main entrance to St Peter Mancroft church, is now part of the pedestrian plaza fronting Norwich's acclaimed new Forum]. They also collected large numbers of bicycle tyres from the Dunlop, Goodyear and Michelin local depots in the city. Bicycles were an important means for ordinary people, and especially workers, to get around so tyres were an essential commodity, especially as they punctured so easily on the rough roads and tracks they had to be used on.

As businesses started to redevelop after the war, Brian remembers the firm picking up many of the local garages as customers. He quickly names a number of them in Wells including; Walsinghams on Warham Road; Roses garage; Mr Guest; Sid Warren; Abels; and Mr Grange who used to do some repairs on Freeman Street, Wells.

"These garages all had a regular requirement for the exchange of oxygen and acetylene cylinders used for oxyacetylene cutting and welding. We used to carry these cylinders backwards and forwards to Plumsteads in King Street, Norwich. Many of the local garages such as Baxters, Southgates and Massey-Bridges, both in Fakenham, also used to ask us to take such items as car seats, radiators and engines for repair in Norwich as this work could not be carried out locally. The car seats were taken to Robinsons on Riverside Road (these days a major car dealership in Heigham Street), the radiators went to Smiths on King Street and the engines which had to be rebored or have their cylinder heads planed used to be taken to Plumsteads or Barkers in Norwich who were the main motor engineers. Much of this type of repair business no longer exists; seats

are much more durable throughout the life of vehicles, radiators are better protected within the vehicle. They are rarely punctured these days and suffer nothing of the effects of adding antifreeze to the radiator's already heavily rusted core and header tank. Car and lorry engines have a much longer life before any stripping down and remanufacture is needed, if at all. I remember also that we carried a great deal of distilled water for the garages and battery acid. This was in glass carboys in shaped metal cages to protect against breakage and I remember them being very heavy and difficult to handle."

The Norwich Rounds
Barkers developed regular routes through the city that were followed for many years. Arriving from Wells they would head first for King Street and make the deliveries and collections they had for that area, and then follow a route that would take them down to Riverside Road, Prince of Wales Road and Magdalen Street. They would then go through the centre of the city and on to Chapelfield. Brian has a favourite memory that characterised these different parts of the old city.

"Each area had its own aroma arising from the various manufacturing and storage operations going on there. The smell that comes most to mind is that of the Chapelfield area where Potters made their 'Perfect Pickles', pickling such vegetables as cabbages and onions. Dunlop had a tyre depot there and, like Potters, is now long gone. But the strong smell of chocolate from Caley's [which later became Mackintosh's and is now destined to be another shopping mall], which I remember very well, remained a feature of that area of the city right up until manufacture of confectionery on that site finally ceased in the 1990s. I always say that if I closed my eyes and somebody had dropped me off in Norwich I would know in what part of the city it was by the characteristic smell.

But Chapelfield was not the only area with its own distinctive smell. When we went down by the old Odeon cinema on Botolph Street there was always the smell from Charles Dix who used to supply most of the butchers with rusk used in the manufacture of sausages, and with sausage skins. Similarly, just as you got near to Botolph Street there was always the smell of baking powder emanating from the firm of De-Carl Smith. Both of these firms were good customers of ours from whom we used to regularly pick up goods for delivery to the North Norfolk village shops. Yet another collection point with a strong 'smell' association was at Dougill and Hastings in Pitt Street who sold leather and Wellington boots. I particularly remember this firm because Mr Derek Hastings of the firm used to stay at my mother's Ostrich House guesthouse in Burnt Street, Wells when he had done his rounds in the area taking orders. We would then collect the parcels from the firm's Norwich depot the next day and deliver them to the various outlets on our return journey."

A Variety of Goods
One of Barkers' main difficulties with such a wide variety of goods to be collected was how best to load them on the lorry. There was very little packaging and certainly no shrink-wrapping of pallets, major features of present distribution operations. And there were no pallet or forklift trucks to help load and unload consignments either. But at least they did not have the worry of conforming to stringent legal limits on axle loadings and fore-and-aft weight distribution that concern transport operators these days.

"When you think that we had to load such items as the oxygen cylinders previously mentioned, new Raleigh bicycles, sometimes as many as twenty or thirty of them at a time, and then Boulton and Paul's rolls of barbed wire, it presented quite a puzzle at times. The cylinders had to lie flat on the floor and not roll about and the barbed wire had to be kept well away from the bicycles, and the other parcels too, so the shiny new paint did not get scratched before the

bike had even reached the cycle shop. We used to scrounge old cartons from some of the places we called at to make a kind of sleeve to protect them from damage. Today, of course, new bikes are transported fully enclosed in protective sheaths. We also collected bikes from the BSA depot behind Chapman's cycle and motorcycle shop in Duke Street [now Michael Powles' car sales showrooms], *but their machines were always sent out in cardboard sleeves, unlike the flimsy brown paper wrap that Raleigh used. Eventually, we got round to carrying old blankets to wrap round the bikes. And with such big mixed loads, frequently we had to make concessions to weight distribution just so the lorry would steer and handle safely on the journey back to Wells."*

As the years passed Brian had gained so much experience in this trade that he claimed he could tell the seasons of the year by the weight on the vehicle and the smell of the parcels. For instance, he remembers the pungent smells of winter loads of rubber boots in great numbers and sheet leather destined for the boot and shoe repair trade, to say nothing of the weight of such loads, the leather in particular. Just about every village had its own local boot and shoe repairer, or cobbler as they were invariably called, who had their supplies of leather delivered in large bales, some weighing as much as three hundredweights. Brian particularly remembers delivering big bales like these to Gower and Reader on Norwich Road, Fakenham. They also carried the heavy-headed hobnails that used to be hammered into farm worker's boots to make the soles and heels last longer. Even boys used to go to school clip-clopping along with the soles of their shoes protected by hobnails and the heels with shaped steel 'Clayton' tips; a far cry from today's designer 'hi-tech' trainer shoes which seem to be the most commonly worn footwear, costly though they are.

Changing times have also seen buckets now being made from plastic, and baths of made enamelled cast iron or fibreglass are built into most homes. In the days of Brian's recollections, buckets were made of galvanised metal and were invariable called 'pails' and, since few houses had built-in plumbing, baths were taken in a tin affair, usually in front of the fire, with the water heated in and bailed from a 'copper' boiler. *"We carried both the pails and tin baths by the hundreds from JBTs in Norwich."* At harvest time the firm used to regularly collect from Wilkinsons vast quantities of the string used in the binders and the slats and sheets for the balers. In winter, sugar-beet forks were collected from JBTs and Thompsons – these were the type with long curved tines which were used to load beet from the side of the road - very heavy manual work for the farm labourer, but now, of course, it is all picked up and loaded with sophisticated machinery that shakes the mud off as well.

By contrast, Leverages on Timber Hill, Norwich, one of Barkers' regular collection points, supplied confectionery, mainly sweets, as did Palmers, usually in large screw-topped jars, which were despatched unsealed and in open-topped cases. As we have already seen, security was not an issue in those days. Similarly, petty theft was not something that fazed Smiths of Magdalen Street who supplied most of the chemist's shops all along the North Norfolk coast and throughout West Norfolk. All the firm's products, whether toothpaste, bandages or medicinal potions, were transported in open-topped boxes with the Smiths name clearly stencilled on the outside, so everybody could guess what was inside. Chemist's shops used to buy the potions in bulk and make up their own medicines behind the counter. For this they needed masses of small bottles which Barkers used to collect for them from Crosskills who were located just behind Smith's Calvert Street warehouse.

A regular Barker customer and a firm still very much in business today, was Looses of Norwich, the china and glass specialists. They used to supply glass Kilner jars for fruit bottling, which was a major household occupation during the war and in the post-war days. Barkers used to deliver these jars to the village ironmongers for sale to the local housewives. Not far from Looses was Coldhams, a firm that supplied most of the hairdressing shops with a wide variety of products. All of these different deliveries used to be made long before the days when the main wholesalers had their own delivery vehicles, so one can imagine the variety of different products that Barkers carried, they numbered dozens and comprised such a complex range of sizes and packing methods, if indeed any packaging was used at all which very often it was not! And all this was before the days when standardisation, 'palletisation' and 'unitisation' came into vogue and vehicle hydraulic tail lifts and roll-cages were years in the future.

Another regular consignment for Barker's was books from Jarrold and Sons of Norwich, one of the firm's biggest customers, who supplied nearly all the schools in North Norfolk. Brian recalls,
"We called every day, as did two or three other local carriers who delivered to other parts of Norwich and Norfolk. The Jarrold despatch bay was located in the basement of their main London Street premises, still a familiar city landmark today, but the snag with this was that you had to go down a number of steps to pick up the orders and sometimes there would be as much as a 3-ton, not tonnes, load of packages to carry up and down these steps. The man in charge, I remember, an ex-Navy man, would stand and watch as we struggled up the steps with our arms full of books, parcelled up with brown paper and string and some weighing three-quarters of a hundredweight, in today's terms that would be around 80 pounds or 36 kilogrammes and probably well above what current-day health and safety legislation would permit a man to carry on his own. The daily load for each individual carrier would be stacked separately so as you hurried down the steps to see what your order was for the day your eyes would sometimes pop open at the size of the consignment. If it was three tons, as it often was in fact, you knew you had a good load for the journey home, especially with all the other consignments you had already picked up. It was a case of turning a blind eye to the maximum weight the lorry was designed to carry or the overloaded rear axle and tyres. Fortunately, weight regulations were not much enforced in those heydays, and after all, business was business!"

Next door in Exchange Street, and today part of Jarrolds' extended retail store, was the old Corn Hall where weekly auction sales were held of second-hand furniture, household effects, books and such like, and on other days, sales of agricultural products. Barkers regularly carried goods both to and from these sales. At Chamberlains too, on Guildhall Hill, well-known wholesaling and retailing clothiers and furnishers in those days, but now sadly long gone, their loading point, like Jarrolds', was on the lower ground floor, so loads had to be carried upstairs to the loading level, although there was a hand-cranked lift that van men could use. This was especially helpful when the load comprised rolls of lino, often weighing some two hundredweights or more each - equivalent to 224 pounds or over 100 kilogrammes. It was impossible for a driver to carry these up the stairs on his own. Curls of Norwich were another shop like Chamberlains. Their despatch point was nearly opposite the Assembly Rooms on Theatre Street on a site where the old city library tragically burned down in August 1994 and the new Norwich Millennium Library and Forum complex opened in November 2001. [Incidentally, this development has almost completely obliterated that part of St Peter's Street where a number of key Barker wholesale customers were located; for example, Reliance Garage, JBTs and Wones.] Curls had the same system as Jarrolds' where the daily consignments for each of the three or four different carriers were stacked in the loading bay.

School deliveries featured largely in the Barker schedules. Besides the delivery of books for Jarrolds, as described above, they used to also deliver dried milk and potatoes, mainly collected from East Anglian Carriers' depot in Guardian Road, Norwich, which was located within the premises of Pointer's Haulage, a well-known local haulage firm.

Barkers had a regular monthly call at Mansfields the cardboard box manufacturers. This firm used to make small boxes especially for Mr Money at South Creake who made razor blades – typical of a small village industry. Brian used to find it particularly fascinating to go into his workshop and see these blades being made and the special machinery operating. The finished blades travelled along an overhead gantry driven by numerous pulley wheels in production-line fashion and were then packed into the small boxes he had delivered. Mention of cardboard boxes brings back more memories for Brian:

"The shoe factories, of which there were many in Norwich, but sadly no longer, were always short of cardboard cartons for packing shoes for despatch. So, with my entrepreneurial spirit, as I went round delivering to different shops I would always be on the look out for suitable cartons and would scrounge these and pack them up during my lunch break. I would then take them back to the shoe factories which would give me three or even six old pence (3d or 6d - equivalent in today's decimal currency to just about 1p and 2½ p) for reasonable-sized cartons.

While this amount may seem virtually worthless by today's values, I saved these small sums, along with other tips I received, and by the early 1950s I had accumulated enough to buy a new Morris 1000 car. I ordered this from Baxters of Fakenham. I remember Mr Piercy, who managed the business, saying to me, "Well young man, how are you going to pay for this car?" I replied, "You get the car, Mr Piercy, and I'll bring you the money", which I did. It cost about £500 as far as I can remember.

At Christmas time in the 1950s many people were very generous to both Fred and me. We used to be given cigarettes as well as money and I can remember taking home enough cigarettes for my father - I did not smoke myself - to keep him going for two or three months at a time without having to buy any for himself."

Going back to the story of the deliveries, another manufacturing plant that interested Brian, although the products were much heavier than the razor blades of Mr Money, was Walsingham Foundry. One building at the foundry seemed to be full of belt-driven lathes and various other pieces of machinery, the belts stretching from floor to ceiling and all driven by a steam engine located at the rear of the building. Brian and his father became good friends with Mr Ralph Howell who managed the foundry. In fact it was through Mr Howell that Barker's were able to obtain an increase in the number of A-licensed vehicles they were operating.

These licences were as scarce as hen's teeth and very costly to buy, if you could even find one to buy. Normally, the only way to obtain such a licence, which was not restricted in the type of goods that could be carried, or the range of operation, was to buy up the business of an existing A licence holder, since the licences could not be traded in their own right without the vehicle and business that went with them. Luckily Leslie Barker was, in fact, able to get one A licence by buying a vehicle complete with a licence from local operator Mr Grange, as Brian describes below.

Brian has other memories of Walsingham Foundry besides the matter of the additional A licence. He recalls that the foundry supplied most of the castings for Laurence Scott and Electromotors, the well-known Norwich manufacturer of electric motors.

"We sometimes had difficulties delivering these into LSE on account of the fact that the firm was highly unionised and the workers controlled the times at which they were prepared to off-load goods. But I got one over them on one occasion. We used to deliver heavy blocks of cast iron from Walsingham, weighing as much as 13 stones each [around 180 pounds or over 80 kilogrammes], and often arrived there just as they were closing for lunch at about 12.30pm. This meant that basically there was nobody around to help unload until about 2 o'clock which caused us a long delay, time that we could not afford to lose. One day I arrived there at about 11.30am and they refused to help me unload until after lunch at around 1.30 to 2pm usually. Feeling in a bit of a mood and not wanting to be messed about, I decided to offload the castings myself despite the struggle to lift that

much weight. And to get my own back on them, I laid them in a line down the yard, turned the wrong way up making them very difficult to pick up. When I got back to Wells father was waiting for me, saying that the phones had been hot with calls from Mr Howell at Walsingham. I had to get over there fast and explain myself. I got a severe dressing down from Mr Howell. But it never happened to me again when delivering to LSE.

Many of the motors made by LSE were going into the Atomic Weapons Research Establishment at Harwell in Oxfordshire and on account of the importance of this work, with Mr Howell's support, we were able to apply to the Traffic Commissioner for an open A carrier's licence. These licences allowed the holder to carry any goods for any customer to any part of the country without restriction. This was our second A licence after the war, the first having been purchased from Mr Grange of Wells who had bought several vehicles with these licences immediately following denationalisation of the state-owned road haulage companies, particularly British Road Services, under the Transport Act of 1953."

It was these two A licences (i.e. the one bought from Mr Grange and the one supported by Mr Howell) that allowed the Barkers to expand their operations into more general haulage. When such licences were granted by the Traffic Area Office at Cambridge, a list of licence grants was published in a regularly-produced booklet called 'Applications and Decisions' [commonly referred to as As&Ds], so all the firm's competitors, and everybody else come to that, knew exactly what licences were held. And even more significantly, they then knew what traffic the firm proposed carrying and who had supported its licence application. This, of course, was well before the deregulation of goods vehicle licensing in the form of O licensing that came into being in 1970.

Despite their newfound freedom to operate further afield, Barkers continued their round of Norwich collections. The lorry would call at R. C. Lee's on the traffic lights at the top of King Street to collect nails for delivery to the building industry. These were delivered to all the small builders in the North Norfolk area, bearing in mind that there were very few large building firms in those days. A little further on from the King Street traffic lights, on the right, was Haggs who specialised in electrical motor repairs and sales, and there were not many days when Barkers did not have an electrical motor to deliver to or collect from there. Both Mr Seeley of Wells and Barnhams of Fakenham, among many others, were both very good customers of Haggs.

Barkers used to give their regular customers a card showing their regular delivery rounds so firms would know which days to consign goods to the various destinations. But the smaller firms, where they did not collect every day, had a card with a large letter B printed on it which was put in a window to indicate to the passing Barker driver that he should call to collect an order. Other carriers had their own cards for display by customers when they had goods to despatch.

Further down King Street was Morgan's brewery from where Barkers used to collect barrels of beer for public houses in their area that had run short. In fact, Brian recalls, that they used to regularly get telephone calls from local pubs when they were short to collect replenishments from all the Norwich breweries. Brewing, of course, was formerly an important trade in Norwich, but sadly no longer are such names as Steward and Patterson, Youngs and Crawshay, Bullards, as well as Morgan's, anything but a distant memory.

"I remember that Morgan's office on King Street was, in fact, a private house where you called with the order before going down to the yard where you had to reverse in off the street on to the loading dock. At Steward and Patterson's I also remember clearly the incredible noise of the heavy steel-shod dray horses on the granite setts in the yard as they manoeuvred for loading or unloading. I also remember at S and P's we were occasionally offered a glass of beer

from the draymen's supply. I usually declined this except when it was very hot in summer. Of course, in those days there were no worries about drink driving laws as there would be today.

Another connection with S and P's was through Miss Barnes, the firm's secretary. Her sisters who ran a sweets and cakes shop in Fakenham were our customers. During her lunchtime, Miss Barnes would go out and buy cakes at Purdy's shop and sweets for resale in her sisters' shop and they would be delivered into a garage in All Saint's Green, Norwich [opposite where the BBC is now located] where we would collect them, the garage doors being left unlocked for us – you wouldn't dare do that today! We used to take these orders to the Fakenham shop, usually loaded on the tailboard and covered with a tarpaulin. What would an Environmental Health Officer have said about that? Fortunately, they weren't around in those days either."

In the same vein, Barkers would often pick up a last minute bale of bacon for one of their shop deliveries from Copemans in Duke Street, the big wholesalers, or from Issac Beers in Oak Street. So this was readily accessible for a quick delivery they used to tie it on to the vehicle petrol tank - something else that, no doubt, today's food hygiene inspectors would have an apoplectic fit about!

Also in King Street was the Oxo depot where collections had to be made following a rash of orders after the local area sales representative, Mr Steward, had called at all the local shops. Brian says that they knew he had called on his rounds by a sudden influx of orders, nearly always to be delivered on the Saturday rounds, this involved calling at up to 100 little shops throughout the Holt, Cromer and Sheringham areas. The rest of these orders would be delivered right along the coast westwards to Heacham and Hunstanton on the following Monday morning.

"You could guarantee that every little shop stocked Oxo cubes on its shelves in those days. But you can be sure that

you wouldn't get today's delivery drivers doing 100 drops in the day, which we often used to do. Talking about the Oxo depot reminds me of a story about our firm's motto, 'Send it by Barker, which we had painted on the front of the lorries for many years. One day, while in the Oxo depot, another carrier's vehicle rolled up to collect orders, it was one of our competitors, and it had 'Send it by... ' painted on the lorry. Father was livid and there was quite a shindig about it."

Brian has already briefly mentioned that the firm carried barbed wire in rolls from Boulton and Paul in Norwich. This famous firm's massive factory was on Riverside where it made everything: wire netting, pig netting, rolled steel joists [commonly referred to by the initials RSJs] used in the building and construction industry, steel window frames for houses and much else besides. During the Second World War it built the famous Boulton and Paul 'Defiant' aircraft and other armaments. Near to Boulton and Paul works was Thompsons, wholesale suppliers of ironmongery. Barkers delivered their orders to such outlets as the Fakenham Hardware Store, to both Crisp's and Rose's hardware shops of Wells and various shops in East Dereham as well as to many other smaller shops around the North Norfolk villages. After collecting in the Riverside area the Barker lorry would move into the city centre, calling at Flittons in Redwell Street, suppliers of cycle and radio batteries. Nowadays, of course, batteries can be readily picked up from the display stands in most shops and supermarkets.

Other collection points in Norwich that Brian recalls were Wilkinsons, the harness makers, opposite the City Hall (mentioned previously) - Powells of Fakenham was one of their largest customers in Barker's delivery area – and Henlys the cable manufacturers supplied electricians in the North Norfolk area. These firms like so many that Brian remembers have either closed down or sold out to other firms, as have people such as Mr George Sealey of Wells who was a regular Barkers customer. Brian recalls the collections they used to make from Tobys the toy firm. This trade was seasonal with large consignments in summer for all their usual delivery towns and seaside resorts, but Barkers also used to deliver much further afield for them, regularly taking full loads each week to the Skegness area in Lincolnshire during the summer time.

The firm of Thorndick and Dawson was yet another regular collection point where Barker's picked up parcels of the familiar old blue sugar bags which shopkeepers bought to fill for their customers. In St Benedict's Street was Douglas Brothers who were in the shoe trade, selling not only boots and shoes, but also leather and other items needed for repairing footwear. There were many other firms selling the same products in those days, but Douglas Brothers was the well-established firm at that time, but sadly no longer existing.

In Charing Cross, where the St Andrew's multi-storey car park stood until demolished in 2002, was the old Norwich City Library [on the corner of Duke Street] and next to it the tram sheds from which the city's last tram ran in December 1935. Baldwin Engineering set up business in the old tram sheds where Barkers used to deliver castings from Walsingham Foundry. Baldwins machined these into finished items. This was long before the firm moved to the outskirts of the city – today there is no longer is a Baldwin Engineering in the Norwich telephone directory. In the same building as Baldwins, Brian remembers a shoe wholesaler called Fletcher Reliant who mostly supplied only the small village shops. Usually this meant a delivery of only one or two pairs of shoes at a time.

Barkers' regular loads weren't only hobnails and castings, books and bikes. Groceries also featured in their collections on a regular basis. Usually demand for these products occurred when local shops ran short of supplies and the firm would be asked to pick up such items as bales of bacon. For example, they used to collect groceries from Burton Saunders in Recorder Road, the orders being mainly for two hundredweight bags of sugar, bales of bacon and tubs of butter. Brian recalls two memorable incidents connected with this firm in his carrier days.

"The first was when driving down Prince of Wales Road, long before it became one-way only, on my way to make a collection; in those days the road was made of wooden blocks which could be very slippery in wet weather and as I got level with Wallace Kings' - the furniture shop, now moved elsewhere in the city - a bus pulled out right in front of me, I braked hard, but the lorry just kept going ... and going ... and going... In fact, it slid right down the wrong side of the central traffic island and, as it was in those days of two-way traffic, on the wrong side of the road! Fortunately for me, nothing was coming up the other way at the time and I didn't hit anything.

My second Burton Saunders experience was quite hair-raising at the time. You have to remember that there was no way of accurately assessing the weight you were putting on a lorry, so we just loaded and loaded until the load-space was filled up, sometimes resulting in a lot of air and not much weight, but at other times we were very heavily overloaded. On this particular occasion we had a big load on board and as I came up Prince of Wales Road to the traffic lights at the bookstall opposite the old Royal Hotel [now a night club with offices above and where the bookstall stood there is now only a closed and sad looking Expresso Bar] the traffic lights turned red so I stopped and yanked hard on the handbrake. Unfortunately, the lever snapped off at the bottom leaving me sitting there holding the vehicle on the footbrake only. When the lights turned green there was no way I could hill-start just on the clutch alone, with a load of that weight on board, without the risk of rolling back. With a number of cars sitting right up to my tailboard I just couldn't afford to let the lorry run backwards so I was in trouble. But just when I needed a policeman, on this occasion one luckily appeared - not like these days, when they are nowhere to be seen unless you've done something wrong, and even then they don't always come! Anyway, he was a big tall sergeant, I remember, with a ginger moustache, and he kindly manoeuvred the following traffic out of the way so I could do a precarious heel and toe start on the hill. Fortunately, I managed it and got myself up to the top of the hill and on to the level of Castle Meadow."

Singer, the sewing machine firm, had a shop and repair facility on Pitt Street in Norwich where Barkers used to drop machines for repair that had been collected from the Singer shops in East Dereham, Kings Lynn and Fakenham, and from individual households. Two or three days later they would collect the repaired machines and take them back to where they had come from. In those days, of course, Singer was a famous name and home sewing was not only a hobby, but also an essential part of everyday life. Brian says,

"Dress making was often the only way for the housewife and her children to have something new to wear, while mens' shirt cuffs and collars were turned as a matter of course and patching up and passing on clothing was the norm – unlike the habits of today's 'throw-away and must have new' trend."

The building trade was the source of many of Barkers orders. Brian quotes as an example Farmiloes in Calvert Street where they used to call to pick up paint and rolls of lead used in roofing. As he says, *"Some of these rolls weighed as much as half a ton and manipulating them on the lorry, by yourself, to make space for other consignments, was quite a feat of strength – but we always managed it!"* Another firm supplying the building trade was Guntons the ironmongers from where they regularly collected goods. Brian particularly remembers that during the war this firm was fire bombed and the night watchman tragically killed. They also collected from many other firms on a regular basis. Shoe firms were regular customers, such as Harmers who supplied clothing and rubber boots, and also blankets. Lamberts on Hay Hill supplied coffee and tobacco and were one of those places with which Brian always associated particular smells. Yet another regular collection was from Wones the greengrocers where Brian remembers picking up crates of oranges when they first became available after the war.

Reliance Garage was a regular customer in the 1950s and 1960s. This was the second garage workshop started in Norwich by the now very large Holdens Motor Group. It is one of the largest, if not the largest, firms of car distributors in the whole of Norfolk with, currently, franchises for Honda, Jeep, Saab and Rover makes. Most of these makes were unheard of when Brian was on the lorry – apart, of course, from the occasional military version of the Jeep seen in Norwich with American soldiers at the wheel. In those days Barkers used to deliver brake drums and other lorry parts into Reliance for repair and then later collect the items for return to their owners.

Another surprising memory of Brian's which illustrates the relaxed attitude about security matters during those times is of the lorry trundling slowly down St Stephen's Street [when it was still a narrow street and before the central barriers and pedestrian crossings were installed], as it did most Wednesdays or Thursdays, and there amongst all the traffic would be a taxi collecting or delivering money from or to Barclays Bank. As he says, there was no Securicor-type firm with armoured vehicles then and the 'loot', as he liked to think of it, was wheeled in or out on flat, open, trolleys for all to see and for any petty criminal to make a grab at and run for it. But obviously that was not considered a likely risk in those relatively crime-free days of the 1950s. Something else that left a strong impression on Brian was seeing apprentices working at Fletchers the printers and paper bag suppliers in Castle Meadow, from whom they used to pick up paper bags and greaseproof paper for delivery to customers in the North Norfolk area. The apprentice boys would be standing against big machines all day long, just feeding one sheet of paper after another into the printing presses. He used to think to himself; *"Thank goodness I'm doing what I am doing rather than that boring job."*

A job that cropped up regularly was the collection and delivery of laundry from and to the lady at Great Witchingham Hall, near

Lenwade, just out of Norwich. She used to send her laundry to the Swan Laundry in Norwich. This was before Bernard Matthews the 'Turkey King' bought the Hall. But when he took it over, Barkers still used to call to deliver books from Jarrolds for Mr Matthew's office and Brian was surprised to see turkeys being kept in cages in the front entrance lobby of the Hall. This was, of course, in Bernard Matthews' early days, but still amazing that the birds should be living in such salubrious surroundings. As Brian says now, in retirement, he learned a lot during his early carrier years! Like, much later for instance, what 'No. 1 talls' and 'A2s' were in relation to the tinned peas and beans, which they started to carry in large quantities for both Smedleys of Wisbech and Lin-Can of Kings Lynn from about the late 1950s. As he quickly learned, No. 1 talls and A2s were the sizes of tins. Another tinned product carried by Barkers was soups for Campbells at Kings Lynn who used to export this product to the NAAFI worldwide via the port of Felixstowe – a very small port in those days, unlike the massive container terminal it is today.

Homeward Bound
After most of the day spent making their Norwich deliveries and collections the Barker crew were ready to set off for home. But welcome though this prospect was after a hard day, it was not a case of a simple 32-mile journey back to Wells. Most days they had to call at Hellesdon, Drayton and Lenwade, then Reepham and Foulsham to make deliveries they had on board for clients in those places before finally making the run home to Wells. Then at 7 am the next day they had to sort out the previous day's collections ready for setting off to Norwich again, delivering the previous days orders on the way. But even the journey itself between Wells and Norwich was not as straightforward as it may sound. Brian has some very clear memories of those journeys and of some scary moments.

"I remember one occasion that has particularly stuck in my mind; we were just leaving Norwich and heading for home when a really thick fog came down very suddenly. This often happened when the weather was much worse than it is today with much more snow and ice and thick fogs making our journey home horrendous. We had no demisters or de-icer

to sort things out and when it was really foggy we used to have to drive with our heads out of the side window to see where we were going. This meant your face and eyebrows getting absolutely frozen and covered in thick ice. In fact, it is hard to describe to people these days how difficult it was to drive about then because, thank goodness, we never see weather like it nowadays, what with the advent of smokeless fuel instead of coal and as a result of strict rulings of the Clear Air Act. Anyway, on this occasion, as we got near to the old Norfolk and Norwich Hospital in St Stephen's Road you really could not see your hand in front of your face. Fortunately I had a van man, Lenny Doy, with me and he got out and walked in front of the lorry all the way from the hospital to the top of Drayton Hill on the Fakenham side of the village. This was quite a few miles he had to walk and I had to drive very slowly before we could see well enough to drive normally and get home safely."

On another occasion that Brian recalls, very heavy snow was the problem. It started falling during the afternoon while they were in Norwich doing their collections and deliveries and continued so heavily that before long there was a 6 to 8 inch covering on the road causing absolute chaos in the city. Deciding that there was no point in trying to continue with their rounds they headed for home. However, after struggling out of the city they were very surprised to find that by the time they got to Lenwade, about eight miles out of the city centre, there was hardly any snow at all. The lorries used to get stuck quite regularly in snow because there was not the traffic to keep the roads clear. Once, when the snow disrupted their journey they spent the night in Mr Asker's bakehouse at North Creake on the way back to Wells via Burnham Market. Talking of roads, those in the Walsingham area deteriorated badly in winter due to the bed of chalk on which most of them were built. This would collapse and lorries would often drop on to their axles. Brian remembers the road from Barsham to Walsingham being particularly bad; it was like running over corrugated sheeting.

Freezing weather that destroyed road surfaces also froze Barkers drivers. Brian recalls that vehicles had no cab heaters in those days, and where the accelerator pedal linkage went through to the engine there was a big hole in the floor that let in a constant blast of icy air. It was not at all unusual for their wet boots to freeze to the pedals when they had to drive for any distance and for the windscreen to be completely iced up ... on the inside. Brian used to carry a potato to rub on the screen to prevent icing and misting up – an old-fashioned remedy that still works well today, if needed.

The weather was not their only obstacle. The lorries themselves frequently let them down with a range of mechanical ailments typical of motoring in those days. For example, punctures were a frequent headache; wheels used to regularly come loose and throttle linkages were forever giving trouble, not to mention many other small and irritating technical problems that frustrated their daily delivery schedules. One frightening occasion that Brian recalls was when they were coming down Grapes Hill in Norwich intending to turn right into St Benedict's Street, but found, at the junction, that they could not make the turn and had to overshoot into Barn Road. On investigation underneath the lorry they found that the steering drag link had dropped off! Not something a modern day truck driver would like to encounter coming down Grapes Hill, that's for sure.

And this was not the only excitement; during the war years when Norwich was being blitzed, it was not unknown for the driver to have to take cover when the sirens sounded. The war actually brought Barkers extra business when Fred used to go regularly to London to collect the furniture and personal belongings of Norfolk people returning home to escape the bombing. Brian remembers the excitement of once going with Fred on one of these trips. He was about 11 years old at the time.

Talking of war time reminded Brian of a canteen in East Dereham where driver Fred Raisborough used to take him to get a good hot dinner for only sixpence or one shilling in pre-decimal money (worth today in decimal coinage 2½ pence or 5 pence). Another war time memory of Brian's was of the tricks he used to play on driver Fred in those far-off days, one of which resulted in Fred sustaining a nasty fall when he moved the rope that Fred used to swing himself up into the back of the lorry.

The London to Norwich wartime household removals were not Barkers only venture into this aspect of the carrying business. In fact, weekend furniture removals, particularly for local farm workers, became a regular job, as the lorries were otherwise standing idle. Some of these were very quick jobs, but others took much longer, when the lorry crew had to lay lino and carpets first before unloading the rest of the furniture. In fact, the firm used to advertise at one time that they undertook furniture removals; as Brian says, they would turn their hand to anything.

The 1953 East Coast Floods

Brian clearly remembers the horrific effects of the 1953 East Coast floods that resulted in considerable damage.

"I was doing the Cromer and Sheringham round on a Saturday and on the way home in the afternoon I got to Salthouse where the wind was blowing a gale. As I got to the bends at the Dun Cow public house the wind blew the lorry on to two wheels, the tarpaulin acting as a sail. Later I took my mother and some of her lady friends over to Holkham where they regularly played cards, and as I was courting a local girl in Holkham village I met her and we went down to the Village Hall where there were activities going on. During the evening somebody came running into the Hall shouting 'Come quick, the water is up on the road.' We ran outside and stood near the Victoria Hotel and looked down Lady Anne's Drive towards Holkham railway station, which was halfway between the beach and the village. The Station Master, his wife and family were standing on the platform waving a Tilley lamp to attract attention because they were completely surrounded by water.

My only thoughts were to get back to Wells to get the lorries out of the garage on Freeman Street. I got in the car and picked up Mother and her friends and set off towards home. The only way back was through Holkham Park, opening the gates to let us through. I dropped off the ladies and came into Wells at the top of the High Street. As I drove down to the bottom of the High Street at Church Plain I could see that it was completely flooded, something we could never have envisaged. Coming towards me through the flood was the local bobby, Sergeant Hewitt, who had his trousers rolled up and his long underpants rolled up over his trousers. He told me I could not get through so I went back via Crown Yard which was deeper even than Church Plain so I turned round and went back to Church Plain, eventually getting through to Ostrich House where Mother lived.

When we got there the headlights shone onto the garden, which looked just like a lake. When I finally got to the garage this too was chaotic. There were dead cattle floating in front of the doors, and the lorries were also floating and trapped against the roof joists. Good job they were, otherwise they'd have floated off out to sea."

Mr Stacey Walsingham, proprietor of a garage in Wells who used to do some of the repairs on the Barker lorries and cars, worked with Brian for two whole days and nights pulling vehicles and boats out of people's gardens and putting things in some sort of order. When they were eventually able to get the lorries free from the building they towed them up to Walsingham's garage and he was able to get them started. But still there were problems. First day out Brian only got a couple of miles when the engine cut out. The filters were blocked in the petrol engine. He called out Mr Walsingham's fitter who came and got the lorry going again, but this went on for a week stopping and starting, and constantly cleaning out filters. What was happening was that the salt water that had got into the petrol tank was reacting on the coating inside the tank. Eventually this was sorted out, but the next problem to arise was with the brakes; the brake chambers had been affected by rust from the seawater. They all had to be renewed over a period of time, but despite these problems Brian recalls that they did manage to keep the vehicles earning which was important.

Pip Reeve rescuing the flood-stranded owners of the Pop-Inn on Wells Quay (Picture:Campbell Maccallum, Wells)

Another of Brian's memories associated with the floods although, he admits, a seemingly quite a small matter now, and not connected with the lorries, but nevertheless major at the time, followed on from the flooding of his mother's home. Ostrich House was on two levels, higher at the front than at the back, and when the floodwaters receded all the mud and filth off the gardens, and from the overflowing cesspits, flowed into the back part of the house.

"*Mother was overwrought with all that was happening, especially because the house was operated as a guest house and she just didn't know what to do. A friend of father's, Mr Dalliston, came down to see what was happening and I remember hearing him tell my father to get himself and my mother away from the house for a day and he would see what he could do. True to his word he cleared it all out – and it had been foul! Then we had the Air Force descend on us with huge blowers, which they used to blow hot air into the house to dry everything out. They did a marvellous job, but even so the house took years to dry out properly."*

The time of the floods was not the only occasion of Barkers contact with the Wells policeman, Sergeant Hewitt. Years earlier, just after the war in fact, when the parliamentary elections were held, Leslie Barker was approached by the local authority to go around to many of the North Norfolk villages collecting the ballot boxes. This was an important job; so important in fact, that Sergeant Hewitt was ordered to travel with the lorry to make sure everything was done properly.

Fleet Build-up
Eventually the Barker general carrier fleet built up to four vehicles and they were providing daily services to Norwich, King's Lynn and Wisbech, with two-way traffic between Norwich and King's Lynn, including a flow of beer which they used to deliver to local pubs,

Marjorie and Leslie Barker in the garden of Ostrich House in 1950.

Ostrich House, Wells before being flooded by the fateful East Coast floods of 1953.

particularly *The Fleece* in Wells where they delivered regularly. The firm's territory covered a line from Wisbech via King's Lynn through to East Dereham and Norwich, then via Aylsham to Holt and Cromer and back along the North Norfolk coast to King's Lynn. They provided a daily parcels collection and delivery service between Norwich, Wells and Kings Lynn and a 48-hour service around the North and West Norfolk towns of Cromer, Wisbech, Swaffham and East Dereham. There was, in fact, a great deal of trade in and out of the smaller towns and villages in Norfolk such as Great Ryburgh, Saxthorpe, Walsingham and East Dereham. Many of them had foundries and Barkers collected and delivered from all of these at different times. Dereham Foundry, for example, made drain covers for the new housing estates that started springing up after the war; they also made wheel hubs that Barkers used to deliver into Alley Trailers at Burnham Market for whom they also used to deliver other goods to Norwich. This was the first firm to make a trailer with a moving floor for 'muck spreading', and they also made tipping trailers that were quite a novelty just after the war. Barkers used to take in wheels and tyres for these trailers that they had collected from the Dunlop depot in Norwich.

The carriage of potatoes, which is to feature more significantly in this story in due course, was a regular aspect of Barkers developing traffic. For instance, the Fakenham nursery, Starks, used to supply many of the village shops with seed potatoes in one hundredweight bags, or sometimes, smaller amounts. This was, of course, seasonal traffic, but for the rest of the year they carried other seeds and plants for the customer.

As the firm expanded, the old shed in the Coach and Horses yard in Orford Place [now Red Lion Street] was vacated and they moved first to a weighbridge shed opposite the old Castle Meadow tearooms and then later took a garage on Timber Hill at Savages the wholesalers. Firms used to still bring goods in to the depot for them to deliver on their rounds. Kerrys of Ipswich, the cycle and motor people were one such client, while Faithfulls of Ipswich would leave consignments of their carpets and tiles for Barkers to deliver.

The End of an Era
Brian's father Leslie died in August 1962 at the age of 62. An obituary in the local paper read:
> *"The funeral of Mr Leslie Sizeland Barker of Shrublands, Polka Road, Wells took place at St Nicholas Church. Mr Barker, who was 62, was in business as a general carrier. He was born in London, moving to Warham as a youth. He set up a business in Wells in 1923 with a taxi and a wood firm and later took on the carriage of goods as part of the business."*

By 1972 Fred Raisborough had retired after 41 years with the firm and this event was also recorded in the newspaper.
> *"A Wells man who has worked with three generations of employers at the same firm received a cheque on Tuesday to mark his retirement. This man was Wilfred (Fred) Raisborough, and he was aged 65 when he retired and he lived in Wells. He was presented with the cheque by Mr Brian Barker of Barker's, the haulage firm, whose*

grandfather was in charge of the business when Mr Raisborough was first employed as a driver 41 years ago."

This news item was accompanied by a photograph showing Brian on behalf of the company presenting Mr Raisborough with a cheque on his retirement after his 41 years' service. Beside Brian stands Mr Webb, who worked for the family and Leonard Reeve - known to one and all as Pip - who also worked with the firm for a long time. Besides teaching Brian to drive as he has already recounted:

"Fred also taught me how to live I would think! He taught me to like music, as he was a member of the Fakenham Town Band, and coming home on the general carrying service at night we often used to pop into the Band Room so Fred could practise. We had many a good night listening to the Town Band.

During the latter part of Fred's employment with the firm, I realised that driving was becoming too much for him and he spent most of his time helping around and doing odd jobs here and there. He was a man who could turn his hand to practically anything. He used to repair shoes as a pastime, not only for himself but for other people as well. He also became a very good gardener who used to look after my mother's garden."

Flood damaged!. Leslie Barker's original workshop from 1928. The old petrol pump is now in Brian's yard

As Barkers moved into general haulage, a new generation of heavy trucks were required. This Commer 'Maxiload' fitted with a Rootes TS3 'blown' two-stoke diesel engine and one of the earliest vehicles to be plated under the 1968 plating and testing regulations, was one such vehicle that served the business well. Driver Jimmy Tottle is on the platform supervising the loading.

The Haulage, Storage and Shipping Years

There had been a tremendous decline in the Barker carrier business through the latter part of the 1960s as a result of dramatic changes in the businesses of many of the firm's traditional clients. For instance, as motor vehicles were becoming more reliable and the concept of component replacement was replacing an era when almost every part of a vehicle was repairable, much of the carrying work between local garages and the main suppliers and repairers in Norwich disappeared. Radiators, batteries and engines all now lasted much longer between repairs, so the demand for the specialist skills of the main workshops in Norwich diminished. Also, new vehicle dealerships were springing up and selling new cars in much greater numbers. At the same time, local garages were able to replace many components with spares from the main dealers or motor parts factors, which they could collect with their own vehicles or have delivered to them directly. Many other Barker clients underwent change too throughout this period, leaving the firm to wonder which way to turn next. Brian recalls:

"As we became aware that the passing trade and general carrying was diminishing to such an extent that we were sending vehicles round with just a few deliveries we decided that we would branch out into long-distance haulage. There came a time when we tried to run both the carrying business and the haulage together, but we were not doing the work properly and it was decided that we would stop the general carrying."

By this time the fleet was up to four lorries and the firm had three full-time employees. It was still doing the Norwich and King's Lynn daily rounds and serving Wisbech, but with Brian ever on the lookout for new opportunities, particularly in long-distance general haulage, the two operations were beginning to run side-by-side. However Brian could see that days of small general carrier were numbered, the future being in specialised bulk haulage, and with this in mind a limited liability company, Barker and Sons (Wells) Limited, was formed in 1962 with Brian, his mother, Mrs Marjorie

K. Barker, and his brother Graham as the first officially appointed directors. The objects of the firm were to operate as road haulage contractors, mainly for bulk and general haulage. From 1964 the firm held a Public A carriers' licence, and by 1967 nine lorries were being operated with eight full-time employees on both the open A and restricted B licences and on a Contract A licence that was issued in 1967. Barkers held contracts with W. Johnson & Son (Long Sutton) Ltd., potato and vegetable growers and merchants, and with Melton Marketing Co. Ltd and others.

As Brian recounts:
"We were one of the very first firms to move into transporting potatoes in bulk using specially-built 'Bulker' bodies on articulated semi-trailers. The tractor units were Commers (powered by the renowned TS3 'blown' two-stroke diesel engine). In fact, we had only the second 'plated' vehicle to come out of the Rootes Group, Commer truck factory at Dunstable in 1967 when the Goods Vehicle Plating and Testing Regulations, introduced under the Road Safety Act of 1967, first came into force."

Licensing Changes

By the beginning of the 1970s, many aspects of the carrier business had significantly altered, not least due to the Transport Act of 1968. This Act wrought many changes to the pre-existing A, B and C licensing system that had existed since the 1933 Act. Carrier licensing was in fact totally replaced by a completely new system of goods vehicle licensing with the introduction of Operator, or as it is more commonly referred to, O licensing from 1970. Gone was the old principle of *quantity* control whereby operators had to prove 'need' with the express support of specific customers to obtain a licence. In its stead came the new concept of *quality* licensing under which safety of operations is the principal criterion to be met for obtaining the grant of a goods vehicle licence by the Traffic Commissioner. This new regime opened the doors to many would-be road hauliers who thought they could see new-found opportunities for making a rich living – a dream that many were disabused of in a very short space of time.

The road haulage industry as a whole has seen many other significant changes too under this post-1970 de-regulated licensing regime. Of particular note has been the development of nationwide 'next day' express parcels services and world-wide courier services enabling customers to despatch goods or important documents on one day with a (in some cases, even, a money-back) guaranteed delivery time one or two days hence. Before noon, before 10 am, and even earlier, delivery promises are commonplace these days. However, despite these apparently highly efficient services, provided by an industry sector bursting at the seams with the latest technology - superior vehicles; mobile communications; on-board computers that link the drivers' cab to the office and global positioning satellite links that can tell the boss where his vehicles are to the nearest metre - the fact remains that from the earliest days of the Barker business they too, both Brian and his father before him, provided regular same day and next day collection and delivery services as their customers demanded.

Reflecting on these licensing changes Brian says:
"I have in front of me an As&Ds booklet [in which applications for new licences and variations and the Licensing Authority's decisions are published] from the Eastern Traffic Area in Cambridge where our licences were issued. In this particular application we applied as Barker & Sons (Wells) Ltd to take over the previous licence held in my father's name, Mr L. S. Barker. This licence permitted us to carry general goods, mainly throughout East Anglia and where required, with a maximum vehicle carrying capacity of 12.75 tons.

As it happens, this application was granted without any bother at all, but there were times when such applications were not so easy. Over time we applied for different variations to our licences and our main objector in those

Late 1960s; the switch over to Commer lorries. Part of the Barker fleet on North Creake airfield, at Egmere.

days was the local firm of T. C. Grange. Mr Grange was, in fact, a very good friend of my father until he died. However, when I used to have to apply for new licences and variation of our existing licences, nine times out of ten Mr Grange would formally object, which he was entitled to do under the licensing laws. Over a number of years, we had both the Public A carriers' licence in operation and a number of B licences under which we used to haul for different named customers. We built up quite a number of these carrier contacts, mainly local people, whose names were actually recorded on the licence. We had dealings with a company called Konskilde, for instance, which came into the country and were supplying farm machinery and we had their name put on the licence, with their agreement.

We were very keen to change these licences into an open A licence. That would allow us to bring back return loads from wherever we were delivering, but the B licence, as I said, was restricted and did not permit this; we could only run loaded one way - outwards. I applied to the Licensing Authority for the B licence to be changed to allow us to bring return loads back into East Anglia. Whether this was complete luck or not, Mr Grange must have been away on holiday or something and did not see this application, and since nobody else objected to the application, it went through unchallenged.

In effect, this made our B licence practically an open-ended A licence. I well remember Mr Grange coming down to see me, and saying 'well, you've done very well and got away with that, and good luck to you.' But at other times I have been along to his office and more or less asked him to withdraw his objection and he would say, "Oh, no, no, no, you're getting too big", or "You're doing this," or "You're doing that, I'm going to let my objection stand." But on most occasions, in fact on all occasions, he would take me up right to the last week and then withdraw his objection. I suppose it was just to keep me in my place. The time I am talking about was mainly round about 1963 when, naturally, we were trying to expand and had to accept work from other haulage companies.

In those days British Road Services, which was still in existence, had local depots in Stowmarket, Wisbech and Ipswich, for example, and I have in front of me a list of the places we delivered to for them. I also notice that we did work for BRS Southampton, and the rate we were paid for the job. Whether this was for a full load or not, I naturally can't remember now, but it was £9.13s.4d [in pre-decimal money]. Another job we did, in November 1963, was for British Road Services from Stowmarket. We were paid £1.9s.3d. The total revenue earned for ten months' work for the King's Lynn depot of BRS totalled only £327.19s.5d. I think this shows how the rates have changed; these figures seem absolutely ridiculous in this day and age [the year 2001]. I have another price list in front of me showing more of our old rates. For instance, we used to do London markets for 36s.9d per ton and loads to Birmingham for 44s.6d per ton. Portsmouth was 55s per ton, Cardiff area 66s per ton, Plymouth 81s per ton and Liverpool 56s per ton. These rates would hardly pay the diesel to get us down the road these days, let alone any of the other costs. I also have in front of me a letter, although unsigned, from the accountants. It reads:

'As requested, I have examined the Company's books for the year ended 31 December 1963 and I have divided the total turn-over for the year between A licence and short-term B licence vehicles. The monthly figures are as follows: The A licence is broken down for the twelve months of 1963 and it comes to a grand total of £10,121. The short-term B licences started in September and operated in 1963 for just four months and came to a grand total of £1,631.'

> *This was probably the time when we realised that we had to apply for these B licences because the work was then increasing and we hadn't got the capacity to cover it all on the A licence and there wasn't much chance of getting a full A licence without considerable problems, or unless we went out and bought one. We did not have the money to do that, so the B licences were the only way round the problem."*

The Strike

Expansion continued and in 1969 Barkers formed a partnership with IFM Road Freight of Halesowen. Both Brian's brother Graham and a Mr Willetts were directors. Unfortunately things didn't go as they should do with Mr Willets and he resigned from the board. Eventually, Barkers took over IFM and as they already had a clearing house in Kings Lynn, manned by Graham Barker, this business was amalgamated with the IFM business to form a new company in August 1972, Barker & Sons (Hauliers – Clearance House Operators) Ltd. [A clearance or clearing house is a firm that takes on haulage work despite having no vehicles of its own. It then subcontracts the work to other independent hauliers taking a percentage cut of the haulage rate paid by the customer.] Prior to this, however, came a disastrous eleven week strike during 1970-71 which culminated in the closure of the haulage side of the business and, in another severe blow to the firm's finances, an implacable demand by the Transport and General Workers' Union for the payment of severance money to the drivers.

Brian recalls the strike with great sadness because it came at a time when the business was making significant strides forward. As he says:

> *"Unfortunately this strike happened as we were gradually building up the haulage company and we had eleven weeks of almost complete stoppage with most of the lorries sitting in the yard. There were two or three exceptions where we had drivers based in Birmingham and King's Lynn who wouldn't strike and they continued to work. Pip Reeve and I each drove a lorry just to keep the wheels turning and some*

money coming in and we were fortunate enough to have fertiliser traffic going into Little Snoring from East Dereham. We used to do two or three loads a day apiece. The strike occurred because the drivers were being paid on a productivity scheme. This meant they got paid so much for each mile run, so much for deliveries made, so much for 'nights out', and payment for any inconvenience that was likely to occur.

The rates of pay had been negotiated when we became unionised. Prior to that we paid the drivers on an hourly rate, but as soon as we went on this productivity scheme the efficiency and the profitability increased, although it did mean the drivers had to keep working. Unfortunately, it appeared that they didn't wish to do this so they withdrew their labour over a weekend. The first I knew about it was when I went down to start work on the Monday morning and found all the lorries in the yard and the drivers standing under the disused filling station canopy next door. I went into the office, but it was a considerable time later before I got to know precisely what their grievances were when Mr Greenough, local representative of the General Workers' Union, came to see me. I wouldn't say he threatened me, but he certainly made it uncomfortable discussing these matters.

I tried to explain to him, and showed him the accounts figures to prove it, that it was impossible for the company to go back to paying on an hourly basis as there was a vast difference between what the drivers were earning and what the company was earning; the profitability when we were running on an hourly-rate basis was non-existent. He wouldn't accept this and said that the drivers would stay out on strike. This saga dragged on and on, finally involving the Department of Employment and Productivity. We had meetings with Mr Greenough and two people from the Department and after eleven weeks, on a Friday, Mr Greenough met me at Freeman Street and agreed that the men would remain on the productivity wage scale and that we would have to sign this up on the following Monday or Tuesday. He said that he expected me to go to Norwich and sign this agreement. I refused and said that I would go half-way to meet him and sign it at Fakenham.

We used the office at Fakenham Employment Exchange and Mr Smith from the DEP and his colleagues came up from London to be there, Mr Smith was going to chair the meeting. As I walked into the room there was Mr Greenough and the two shop stewards from the company. Mr Webb came with me to represent the company, but before I had even sat down Mr Greenough turned to me and said, 'What we agreed on Friday the drivers won't accept.' I replied to the effect that he had assured me that everything was all right and we should start back to work this week. His answer was that they were going to be on strike for another week until they had a new agreement. I said that I would like to make a telephone call. I rang my brother Graham and we had a long conversation. He said, 'Do what you feel is right and I'll back you'. So I went back into the meeting and told Mr Smith I had decided, with my brother's agreement that we would close down the transport side of the business. Mr Greenough jumped up and said 'this can't be done. I would like to speak to my shop stewards.' I said, 'Well, whatever you say, Mr Greenough, on the basis of the agreements that we have had and the way you have put in your extra claims we are going to close down the transport side of the business.' He said to Mr Smith, 'Can we have a meeting outside with my shop stewards?' Mr Smith agreed and asked if I would be good enough to wait.

When they came back in Mr Greenough said that it had been agreed that the men would accept redundancy. I replied to the effect that I wouldn't make redundancy payments as I wasn't making them redundant. I had written to each driver individually, and had guaranteed them all six months' work and they had withdrawn their labour. Mr Greenough replied that if this was the case, we shall still put pickets out and we shall picket your office at King's Lynn and we shall see that you never do another day's work out of King's Lynn. Your warehouse companies at Little Snoring will be picketed and we shall put a picket on your front door.' This really knocked the wind out of my sails and I said that I wouldn't pay redundancy, but after discussion with Mr Smith, he said, 'I would advise you to see if we can change the wording and you pay severance pay.' This was done, and the transport side of the business closed down in December 1970.

As the weeks progressed five drivers ask to return initially and within seven weeks, all but two of them wished to return to work. I must say that this strike hurt me very much. I had felt that I had an understanding with the people who were representing the drivers and also had their interests at heart, but as soon as Mr Greenough of the Transport and General Workers' Union came on the scene everybody seemed to think that he could wave a magic wand and produce money that wasn't there."

The Storage Years
In the early 1970s, despite the hassles and disruption caused by the haulage strike, the Barker company was being approached by firms to store goods, mainly agricultural produce and other commodities, so it rented a hanger at Little Snoring Airfield initially for eighteen months, later taking on another hanger when the opposition looked like following suit. Brian was running the Wells office and looking after the storage operation at Little Snoring. Looking ahead, both he and brother Graham could see the likely potential offered by the coming of the Common Market and the likelihood that shipping into Wells would increase, so another company was formed in August 1974 to handle shipping through the port of Wells. This company, Barker and Sons (Shipping) Ltd., was run by Mr W. G. (Bill) Newstead, an experienced shipping manager, Brian and brother Graham were also directors.

The early 1980s saw flourishing traffic through the warehouse and shipping business and from then on most of the haulage work was put through the clearing house operation, which was a follow-up from the decision to close the haulage operation after the 1970 strike. As the trade in both warehousing and shipping increased, so it became necessary to put the lorries back into operation. Over a period of time the company decided to try to purchase the two Little Snoring warehouses and formed a company called Fakenham Warehouse and Storage Company in July 1971 for that specific purpose.

Brian explains that the need for forming these different limited liability companies, particularly the main one, Barker & Sons (Wells) Ltd, which was formed on 31 December 1962 was to protect against tax liabilities in the event of his mother's death. Mrs Marjorie Barker was then in her late seventies and it was obvious that without positive tax avoidance action it would be likely that death duties would cripple the business and probably close it down.

All the accounting was done in Freeman Street where Barker's had an office with two or three young ladies dealing with the accounts. In charge of this operation was Mr Webb, who had been in the haulage industry with local firms T. C. Grange and subsequently Rickwood Brothers, which eventually took over Granges. When Rickwoods finally closed in Wells, Mr Webb joined Barkers and stayed for a number of years. When he came up for retirement Mr Ray Smythe joined as office manager and looked after the accounts and general administration. Day-to-day management control of the business was divided. The clearing house operation was run from the King's Lynn office by Graham Barker, the shipping activity was run by Bill Newstead, while Brian himself controlled the Fakenham Warehouse and Storage business and both the garage and transport operations, although at different times there were other people managing staff at the warehouse.

No 1 warehouse at Little Snoring airfield – Smedley's garden peas and other products awaiting distribution.
(picture: Henk Snoek)

Storage was a volatile business, fluctuating almost by the month; one month inundated with work and then two or three months when nothing would be heard from a customer. It depended mainly on the seasons and on whether customers had over-produced. As Brian says:

> "Over a period of time we had many different companies that were very pleased to put their work our way. In turn the warehouse helped both the haulage side and also the clearance house side, which naturally had first refusal on the work in and out. It also helped the shipping because the number of cargoes that went up into the Little Snoring warehouse was quite considerable. A good example was imported soya and fishmeal - a foul-smelling commodity giving rise to complaints from people on the quay - that went into temporary storage prior to final delivery."

When the shipping container revolution came along, the business had a storage contract with major container and trailer manufacturer, Crane Fruehauf [now General Trailers], which had factories at East Dereham and North Walsham. This firm manufactured containers for the big OCL and Sealink shipping lines as well as other container companies. Since the newly made containers could only be shipped out when the new container ships were completed, Crane Fruehauf had to find storage for them in the interim. Little Snoring airfield was an ideal place for this so they used to store them there, on the perimeter track adjacent to the Barker hangars, as many as 500 at a time, prior to being transported to Liverpool and Southampton. This business carried on for some eighteen months and was a boon both for Barkers and for a lot of other hauliers within the area.

In the early 1970s, the firm was fortunate to obtain a job to haul one-hundredweight bags of potatoes for Smith's Crisps on behalf of Beeson and Whisker, the potato suppliers. From that time they used to deliver to Smith's Crisps' factories at Southampton, Manchester and many other locations in England. Around this time, many of the potato firms in Lincolnshire were starting to use bulk loading trailers and not wishing to lose out on this burgeoning trade, Barkers felt they had to follow suit unless they were to risk losing all the business. Thus they purchased five specially built 'bulker' bodies, which, as was the common practice, were strapped to the flat platform trailers. Three of the bodies had endless belts and the other two had chain-driven belts. Brian again recalls:

"We had two and a half very good years with these vehicles, working them all season and then we were able to use the three belt-driven bulkers for carrying other products such as onions, coal, in fact anything that could be run on these belts. So for the three years that these bulkers were operating they made us a reasonable profit or, I would say, a good profit. During this time we were also doing a very big tonnage of potatoes in half-hundred-weight bags to the London and Midland markets, but this meant that, bearing in mind where we were situated out on a limb on the North Norfolk coast, we couldn't afford to run the vehicles back empty, so we started to build up contacts that would supply us with back loads. This worked quite well in the Midlands, where, through our warehouse company and our association with Norfolk Canners at North Walsham, we were also able to run to Birmingham. We took over an office there that was a remnant of our IFM haulage days and we were running as many as four or five lorries a night delivering HP Beans to the Aston area of Birmingham. From there we would run down to Halesowen and reload back to East Anglia. This was very good trade for us."

Unfortunately, these good days were not to last. When the bulk potato trade was at its height Barkers had a job to match the competition, especially when the big hauliers started to slash haulage rates to uneconomical levels. So they switched to grain carrying, barley mainly, up to the docks and to the brewers in the Midlands. The existing bulkers were still suitable for this work, and in fact, the fleet had increased to five or six articulated bulker vehicles. They also ran a couple of eight-wheel bulkers on local work that proved to be quite good, especially at harvest time. These eight-wheelers were quite easy to find work for, as Barker's had several customers in the area needing such vehicles. For example, they used to carry quite a lot of stone, for Redlands and Wimpeys and those types of building and construction firms. Coupled to that, when the shipping activity was in full flow, they managed four or five loads a day from ships in Wells harbour to the Little Snoring airfield warehouse as well as outward deliveries from the warehouse for storage clients.

Brian remembers these times particularly because this was when Britain's new motorways were beginning to open up.

"When we were doing the HP Baked Beans job to Aston, Birmingham, this was when the M1 motorway through Northampton was newly opened and we had at least a year or 18 months of nightly tyre problems. Blowouts and treads being blown off were common. Treads would actually roll off the tyre casings due to the excessive speed the vehicles were capable of, and at which the drivers insisted on driving them with no statutory limit to observe. The tyres we were using just could not stand up to motorway stresses. We used to experiment with the tyres to find which were the best and we came to the conclusion that if we fitted Michelin Xs [a very popular type of radial truck tyre of the day used by many haulage firms] *we would have no more problems. I suppose being French made for use at higher sustained speeds on their* autoroutes *than we are used to in England. We used these Michelin Xs on both tractor unit drive axles and on the trailers. However, on the trailers, they were OK except when running the bulkers back empty when we had endless problems because, with just the empty bulk body to carry, they were not heavy enough to prevent the axles bouncing and causing excessive and uneven wear on the tyres. We had no end of people come down to examine both the trailers and the tyres, even Michelin's representatives came down with the Crane Fruehauf trailer people. In the end we all realised that the problem was due to the axles of the trailers being set so far back that when the driver braked hard the wheels bounced up and down on the road causing a flat spot on the tyres. From then on, each time this occurred,*

nine time out of ten, the flat spot would be the one that would hit the ground and make it progressively worse and worse. We had to think again about this as there was no ready solution to the problem and the only way we could get out of it was to get rid of that type of trailer and replace them with others of more suitable design where the axles and wheels were set further in from the rear end. This solved the problem for us and we suffered no more excessive scuffing of the tyres."

Progressively, the firm went back into haulage after the 1970/71 strike, but it was not a calculated move on their part. They started off with two eight-wheel lorries which were put to work helping to discharge the vessels that were bringing soya and other commodities into Wells harbour. It was becoming increasingly difficult getting suitable transport to cover the work on the dates of ships' arrivals so they gradually crept back into haulage to ensure they could cover the work. The fleet expanded year by year in the 1980s as they found that the two eight-wheelers were not able to cope with the all the work that was being offered, especially bulk agricultural loads from farms or other bulk deliveries into Seamans', Dalgety and Eastern Counties Farmers. They also found that the fertiliser trade in the area was increasing. At around this time they had several thousand tons of fertiliser stored in the Fakenham warehouse, as well as grain, which was hauled in as an overspill from Dalgety. Thus it was that Barkers the general carriers had become Barker's road hauliers to the agricultural industry.

During the 1980s, which was a boom time for the warehousing operation, they experienced changes of policy among their customers who were storing a variety of commodities. Also, as the UK became more involved with Europe, the rules and regulations being laid down about what could be stored and how it had to be stored were beginning to have an effect on the business that was being put through the Barker warehouse. Although the firm's regular customers, such as British Sugar Corporation, and the odd grain company during harvest-time, continued using them, they realised that the whole aspect of the warehouse business was changing. Brian says:

"It then meant that we had to go out and find something else to put into these hangars and I met one or two people who were handling Intervention Grain. I first went to see a Mr Pledger at Shipdham and looked at his warehouse. Mr Pledger was in the haulage industry at one time [and the co-author's boss in his early days with British Road Services] *and had decided to open up his warehousing for the storage of Intervention Grain for the government.* [NB: The government bought up all the surplus grain produced as a result of improved farming methods and prodigious use of fertiliser, stored it and controlled its distribution via the 'Interventions Board'.] *He in turn put me in contact with Mr Adrian Rutterford who had numerous stores over the country and he advised us how to set up an Intervention Store. It wasn't very straightforward. This involved a considerable amount of work and I had numerous meetings with the bank regarding funding for the grain walling, equipment to dry the grain and a weighbridge to weigh vehicles in and out, and on top of this we needed a laboratory to test the grain when it came into the warehouse. We did set it up and the first year the grain came in and the building was completely full. We emptied it by about 50 per cent and it was then filled up again. Two years later the government changed its policy and decided to stop storing Intervention Grain. So they cleared out everything that we had in store. Fortunately, we were able to pay off all that we had borrowed for setting up this project and we ended up with a warehouse that had grain walling and all the equipment to maintain the quality of grain that we had in store. We then set about trying to persuade local companies to store grain with us. Although we didn't achieve the volume that we'd previously had with the Intervention Store we were at least able to store quite considerable quantities of grain. In fact, during harvest time, we used one warehouse completely for grain and half of the second one.*

The story of our two hangars at Little Snoring hangers was initially quite a sorry saga. We originally took them on lease from the owners who had used them for housing and rearing cattle. Each was divided into four sections with block walls. I remember going into these buildings one weekend and knocking down all these dividing walls and breaking them up into rubble to use for in-fill. The sorry saga related to what had happened to the cattle; during the hot and humid weather they had sweated and their perspiration had formed condensation on the roof of the buildings and then water dropped down onto them and they got pneumonia and died. At this point the owners realised that the buildings were not suitable for rearing cattle, and this is why we were able to obtain our lease on them.

Within a short time of taking on the lease, the company that owned the buildings decided it wished to sell them. But then another problem arose insofar as the owners intended to put them out for tender. Although, as I've said, we were doing well at that time, we were a little nervous that we might lose out, so we decided to put in a tender as well. Fortunately, our offer was accepted and that is how we purchased the buildings through our Fakenham Storage and Warehouse Company."

As with most property a certain amount of maintenance work had to be done and on these two vast hangars the roof was one of the major problems. This was particularly so due to the fact that they were situated, in a very exposed location liable to catch the wind. The corrugated sheeting used to lift, allowing water to get in, which caused numerous problems. The roof had to be re-sealed, and there were also problems with the doors, mostly caused through water. In fact rain water, condensation from the cattle and the dampness from the straw bedding all drained into the staunchings of the building, which were becoming eaten away with rust.

Periodically the firm had to call in Wensum Engineering to carry out major repairs. Brian remembers these being very costly. The roadway between the two hangars was yet another problem. This was over private land belonging to a Mr Cushion, although there was a right of way for the use of the buildings and to the local flying club using the airfield. However, over a period of time with heavy vehicles going backwards and forwards, the concrete, which had been laid during the war, started to deteriorate and holes appeared. As Brian recalls, Mr Cushion got a little annoyed and in the end they had the further considerable expense of laying an asphalt road. This road carried a lot of traffic, not only Barker's own lorries, but the vehicles of specialist repair firms such as those brought in to service forklift trucks and the blowing equipment for the grain, as well as Barnham Electrical and another local firm which looked after the electric motors.

Besides the Little Snoring warehouse operations, Barkers also had storage facilities at the old lime works site in Wells in which a Mr Parsons was interested. During the 1980s Mr Parsons had set up his mixing plant from which he used to supply the farming industry with fertilisers. Some farms collected their own supplies from the store, but Barkers and other haulage firms also used to haul outward loads from the site. Brian says:

"We found when we started this work, and for some considerable time afterwards, that this business was quite profitable insomuch that two or three of our companies were being used in this project. Firstly, the shipping company had the job of discharging the ships and looking after the agencies with the vessels, secondly, the haulage from the Quay to the lime works was mainly on our own fleet, and thirdly, the property and land that the Parsons Company used was invoiced through our Fakenham Warehouse and Storage Company. Mainly, this was all bulk material, but at different times we also stored bagged fertiliser at the lime - works. When we first took over the site all the old buildings used in the lime manufacturing were still standing, but over

a period of time we knocked them down, levelling off areas, so the land could be used for other purposes."

Eventually, another catastrophe hit at the heart of the Barker family business when three big customers pulled out of their warehousing contracts on the collapse of the fertiliser trade due to environmental pressure on farmers to cease crop spraying. In consequence of this the hangars were sold, the first one in September 1990 and the second one in October 1994.

The Shipping Boom

As time progressed, especially in the 1970s, more and more ships were visiting the port of Wells bringing in different commodities, mainly for the farming industry, and a large percentage of this being fertiliser. After the war, Mr Grange and Eastern Counties Farmers, which had a branch in Wells, used to import kainite [a salt-based fertiliser that played havoc with lorries, corroding the metalwork] for the sugar beet crops. This was an ongoing commodity that continued to be imported right up till the end of the 1980s. Bagged fertiliser was brought into the port on behalf of Shell UK, BASF and a number of other companies. Initially, consignments used to arrive loose in the bottom of the ship and the bags had to be handled manually on to the lorries once the crane hauled them out of the hold onto the quay. Unloading at the store or farm destination was by the same means, manually. In time, Barker's adopted more mechanised systems and palletised all loose loads within the ship's hold so they could be craned out onto the flat beds of the waiting lorries and unloaded at the store by fork lift truck. There was still a certain amount of loose fertiliser coming in and Brian thought he could see a market for bagging this up, so he contracted with a local engineering firm, Wensum Engineering at Fakenham, to come in and manufacture an on-site bagging plant at Little Snoring – this was later moved to the Wells lime works site. This worked quite well, and to take a step further the firm thought that they would like to have a warehouse a little bit nearer to Wells. Brian continues:

The beginnings of mechanisation: unloading fish meal from ship to pallet on Wells quay.

"We went through all the different financial schemes available, with the bank and with the agricultural finance people, to erect a building which would be used mainly for grain storage. We saw this market hopefully developing as an export business for barley and we also felt that we could store fertiliser there and cut out the ten miles to and from the Fakenham warehouse.

As time progressed Mr John Parsons of Parsons Marketing at Fosdyke used to bring in the kainite boats and he could see that there was also a market for other fertilisers, which he started to bring into the harbour. We found that if we were not careful we could lose the haulage traffic to Little Snoring and revenue from the extra handling involved. Anyway, a warehouse was erected at the old lime works on Holkham Estates' land and put into use. It then became obvious to Mr Parsons that he needed a larger outlet at Wells and he put a proposition to us for renting some of the buildings, or a building plus the weighbridge at the lime works, and erecting a building of his own for bagging up. He did this, and it continued for a number of years."

Wells' sea-borne imports were coming in mainly from Germany, Holland and Denmark - feeding stuffs and fertilisers - and timber occasionally arrived from Sweden. The main exports were peas and beans and one of the key imports in the 1980s was Danish and Faroes herring meal, which was brought in by coasters such as the motor vessels *Tramp* of Aalborg and the *Orthonia* of Odense. At a ceremony in March 1981, a presentation of a painting of Wells Harbour by a local artist, Mr Jack Cox, was made to Captain Francis Moeller, skipper of the *Tramp,* in recognition of the vessel's fiftieth visit to the port. In return, Mr Moeller, who said that they were always given a warm welcome and dealt with expertly by Barker & Sons Shipping [in fact, Barker's records show that the ship visited Wells eighty times over a six year period], presented Mr Newstead, a director of the company, with an engraved plaque of the *Tramp*. The

Presentation to Captain Francis Moeller, skipper of *Tramp*. From the left: Captain Moeller; Boy Court, Wells Harbour pilot; Bill Newstead, Director, Barker Shipping Co.; Brian Barker and Mrs Myrtle French, Chairman of Wells town council.

ceremony was attended by; Mrs Myrtle French, the Council Chairman; the port pilot, Boy Court; plus Brian Barker and Bill Newstead representing the Barker shipping company. This event was quite a landmark both for the town and for the Barker business. Brian recalls that the town was very pleased that Captain Moeller had married a local girl, who was the daughter of Mr David Cox, the then coxswain of Wells lifeboat, and who still lives in the area. Unfortunately, the *Tramp* sank on 5 June 1983 on one of its later sailings to the UK - its 4-man crew were rescued by another vessel.

As sole shipping agents at Wells, Barkers were trying to build exports for ships leaving the port empty having brought in such cargoes as fertiliser and animal feeding stuffs. The port's heydays were the early days of the 1980s. In fact, 1980 was a record year with 161 vessels recorded as entering the port.

The *Eastern Daily Press* reported another port record as follows:
'Wells port record.
A port record was established at Wells before the Easter holidays with a speedy unloading and reloading of a vessel. Last Thursday, the motor vessel Nettie, *which had arrived on the previous evening's tide, began discharging 330 tons of cereal replacer pellets at 7am. She had completely discharged that cargo and loaded 287 tons of feeding peas by 6.30 pm the same day and sailed on the evening tide.'*

Brian responds to this report by saying:
"It was always our objective to give vessels a quick turnaround whether unloading or loading, but it was an added bonus when we handled vessels with two cargoes in the same day."

Cereal pellets, mentioned above, were one of the cargoes that provided Barkers with quite a large trade, but they also handled shiploads of tapioca, which presented the firm with particular problems. This cargo was very dusty and if the prevailing winds were from the east or north-east they had the problem of dust flying

Wells harbour enjoys one of its busiest times ever.
(Picture: EDPpics)

everywhere, not just on the quayside, but much further away. Brian recalls:

> "We unloaded two or three shiploads of this stuff and we often had to stop because the dust was flying all over the properties along the front of the quay and, naturally, there were complaints. As we did not wish to offend the owners of these properties we used to stop the discharging, but the damage was sometimes done as the crane drivers and men who were discharging the vessels obviously wanted to get on with the work and earn their money. After considerable thought we decided to try to erect a barrier to stop the tapioca from flying onto the front. We spent well over £1,000 making and erecting the poles and getting the sheets to screen the lorries so the stuff didn't blow along the quay. Sometimes it worked, sometimes it didn't. But at least we tried."

Another project connected to the harbour was in conjunction with a Mr Hingley, who operated a small coaster which he used to dredge for shingle. Brian again:

> "This shingle was taken to our site at the lime works and put through a screening plant where it was washed and sorted. Unfortunately, this was very much of a hit and miss job. There was always some reason that you couldn't plan for certainty. Either the ship would not be back alongside to discharge, or with the salt getting into all the moving parts of the screening plant there were numerous breakdowns. Besides which, the aggregate companies wanted the shingle for nothing, we had to haul it, Mr Hingley had to recover it from the harbour and sort and wash it and then it had to be delivered to the aggregate customers. There was not a lot of profit in that for us, only a lot of hassle."

The largest ship ever to bring a cargo into Wells harbour was the Panama registered *Vitanova*. It was 187 feet long and had a net registered tonnage of 378 tons. She brought in 400 tons of herring meal in bags from Norway. This all went into the Fakenham warehouse. The port activities created quite a lot of interest for the local townspeople, for those coming in to do their weekly shopping and for the holidaymakers. Brian recalls:

"On numerous occasions I had to go to the ships with the ship's papers or to see a discharge was going OK and people would come up to me and ask when such and such a ship was due in the port and what cargoes we had coming in. I feel it also helped the shopkeepers within the town as we were probably handling most of the ships' agencies that came into the port and it meant signing cheques for the commodities that they purchased, drawing cash from the bank to pay ships' crews and such like. Quite a considerable amount of money was drawn for them on the day they arrived."

In March 1975 Barkers were asked if they would accept a vessel from Sweden that was bringing timber boles (tree trunks) into Norfolk. This vessel was originally due to go into King's Lynn, but for some reason that Brian was not aware of, it was decided to try Wells harbour instead. This turned out to be less of a blessing than Brian imagined because, as he found out later how very difficult it was to gauge the weight for loading on to the vehicles, which was worrying because of the stringent rules governing vehicle weights on the road and the heavy fines that were imposed on convicted 'overloaders'. Brian recalls that they had quite a job getting the timber out from the hold of the ship, particularly as some of it was banded and some of it was loose. The banded wood proved to be quite easy to handle, apart from the fact that they never knew what weight was loaded on the vehicles and unfortunately, Brian confesses, they did have vehicles leave the port carrying more weight than was legally permitted. The firm handled two of these vessels, but as they shipped only about 200-250 tons of timber at a time this turned out to be uneconomical for the shipping company and the trade was stopped.

Another commodity that Barker's actively canvassed for was coal and they were successful in arranging two shiploads into the harbour. But this trade too met an unfortunate end because on arrival of the second cargo of coal, the Yorkshire coal miners' strike hit the headlines. As Brian says:

"We had to decide what was best for the town as the vessel was sitting at anchor outside the harbour, near the fairway buoy, waiting to come in. We heard from King's Lynn that miners were on their way to picket the port of Wells and we thought that, as an open port with an open quay, it would offer no security. I was worried that if the police became involved they would not be able to control the area and the town would suffer the consequent problems so, unfortunately, we had to turn this vessel away and it went down to Mistley in Essex [on the River Stour] *and discharged on a closed quay. After that all the coal shipments went to Mistley so we missed out completely.*

As I look through more old records I can see that on 24 September 1982 Wells harbour enjoyed one of its busiest days ever with eight ships in the harbour. Of these Favor Parker had two soya bean shipments for the silos at the East End Quay and we handled the other ships. But in time, during the latter part of the 1980s, our haulage operation was helping to discharge Favor Parker ships as well as those that came in on our account. Our shipping company worked extensively for Favor Parker who I feel can be justifiably credited with what was the start of a boom when the volume of ships that came into Wells harbour really increased. It was a coincidence that we expanded too, and were able to bring in vessels around the same time. It was a really marvellous sight to see the harbour busy and the ships lying side-by-side at the quay.

But the shipping business was not all roses. We certainly had our problems. For instance, on one occasion I remember that a mooring rope holding the bow of one of the vessels sheared. The rope had been secured through a ring on the quay with a baulk of timber pushed through it as a

The King's Lynn office with Graham Barker (top picture), Bill Newstead (in lower picture at rear) and Paul Lascelles

tensioner. But that night, the tide was so strong that it snapped this four-by-four piece of timber which then flew into the air and over the top of houses on the quay and landed in Mrs Abel's yard. On another night we had a major scare when vandals cast off a coaster from its moorings. The vessel swung round crushing the stern of the Wells pilot boat and nearly scuttling a number of moored cruisers on which holidaymakers were sleeping. It was only by luck that the ship did not end up at the east end of the harbour. Whatever would have happened if she had broken away completely, nobody knows. She would probably still be lying there now!

The difficulties were not only with the ships, even lorries caused us grief from time to time such as in May 1979 when for the second time a vehicle overturned on the quay, fortunately, it was not one of ours. This occurred while loading a ship for the British Sugar Corporation. What appears to have happened was that the pulp nuts [a by-product of the beet used in sugar processing which was used for animal feed], *coming up from the Bury St Edmunds sugar factory, had probably been loaded overnight while still warm causing, it to stick in the vehicle body and difficult to discharge onto the elevator. In this instance the lorry had discharged three-quarters of its load and all the weight was left hanging at the very top of the body which was at the full extension of the tipping ram and, being completely off balance, over she went. We had had a similar experience in the warehouse on a previous occasion and orders had been given to staff and checkers that they were to monitor all loads within vehicle bodies because of the dangers. Obviously to no avail as this later event showed!"*

As the years progressed the company tried to increase the volume they were handling through the port of King's Lynn. There were regular shipments for John Parsons, Eastern Counties Farmers, and Dalgety, who also shipped in material via Norwich. Barkers had had vessels in at Wisbech port too, but decided that the next operation would be King's Lynn. They already had a company office at King's Lynn operated by Brian's brother Graham. He was approached by Wimpey Aggregates based at Pentney, which was in turn were working for a Lowestoft firm called SLP which manufactured mastic mats for the oil industry. This firm had a contract to supply shipments to Norway with the material being made at Wimpey's plant at Pentney. Barker's counted themselves very fortunate to win this contract because not only would they be doing the road haulage from Pentney to King's Lynn docks, but they would also be handling the ships' agency business and taking responsibility for loading the ships.

At about the same time, British Sugar Corporation started to export pulp nuts for animal feed out of King's Lynn. Barker's had been doing a few vessels for BSC from Wells harbour, but progressively the tonnage out of King's Lynn started to increase and this was good business for them. In fact, over a number of years they were handling close on 100,000 tons annually for these two clients, which was a very creditable achievement for their small company.

Unfortunately, as in so many other cases, these good times came to an end. Both of these customers changed their company policies within a 6-month period. The SLP venture finished because the firm decided to export its shipments through Lowestoft, while BSC closed its factory in King's Lynn and from then on exported through the ports of Great Yarmouth and Ipswich. As Brian says:

> "This was a very big blow at that time. The last letter I had from British Sugar Corporation, in fact it was from their subsidiary company Trident Feeds, reads as follows:
>
> *'Review of port and agents performance 1993/94 campaign.*
>
> *This year the tonnage that was shipped through King's Lynn fell dramatically because of the closure of our factory there and our subsequent decision to ship products through Great Yarmouth. However, the 3,000 tons which was handled by yourselves was handled in your normal efficient manner. All our*

instructions were carried out and we have no instances of contamination of the product that you handled. We therefore received no claims. Again, a satisfactory performance.'

That letter meant a great deal to us. We like to accept the praise, but it did mean the end of our shipping activities. We had those two blows and never recovered from them. As I have mentioned earlier, the amount of money that was spent in the town of Wells by the crews and the owners of the ships that came into the port was quite considerable. Another thing I remember was that during our booming years of the 1980s, every Christmas we used to go to a different restaurant or public house that served Christmas meals for our firm's annual Christmas party. We used to average 30 or more people on the staff and we got a great deal of pleasure to think that we were supporting the other businesses locally, as well as enjoying the event."

A far cry from Model 'T' Ford truck his father used to start the business, this 38-tonner with the family name emblazoned on the trailer was Brian's pride and joy.

Foden 8-wheeler bulk tipper with driver Geoffrey Waites.

Chris Barker supervises the loading of chippings for road surfacing.

Wash down: driver Malcolm Raisborough gives the Mercedes bulk tipper a clean down.

Eddie Trett displays his physique, or is he showing off his load of mastic before it is off-loaded to ship.

The Final Years

At this point Brian introduces into the story key employee Mr Leonard (Pip) Reeve who joined Barkers as a mechanic from the local firm of Abel's Coaches. From this time on they were able to do their own in-house maintenance on the lorries. Pip was a person who could turn his hand to anything asked of him, not only vehicle repairs, but also driving, so that when a driver went sick, or failed to turn up for work, he would fill in to keep the wheels turning. Although initially employed only on an after-hours basis from his daytime job, eventually the fleet became large enough for him to be employed full-time. Brian continues:

> *"When we had the strike I did mention that the filling station next door was closed up and BP, the petrol company, had crazed us to run the site. We discussed this, my brother and myself and Pip Reeve, and we came up with the idea that if we could use Mr Reeve's mechanical expertise we could set up a repair garage. We also thought that the way to bring cars in would be to have a filling station. Pip would run the garage, as I didn't have any expertise in repair work, and he would be responsible for that while I would oversee the filling station and the paperwork for the repair work. The garage business went very well for a number of years, being open seven days a week. We built a new workshop on Freeman Street, Wells, in 1978 to Ministry of Transport standards, being a fully equipped, 60 ft long by 40 ft wide, service and repair facility for cars.*

The opening of the garage was celebrated with a full-page feature in the Eastern Daily Press of 11 July 1978. The article describes how the workshop was designed for private vehicle MOT testing and equipped on the advice of Ministry officials to meet the higher MOT standards which were about to come into force, including the provision of brake testers and a lubrication bay. The article describes how the experienced fitters employed also work on the haulage vehicles and do some work on ships in Wells harbour when needed. The newspaper described the new facility as being important for

Wells and the neighbourhood and typical of the forward-looking policy of the Barker Company, by which it is determined to offer customers the best service available.

The garage had had a chequered history before this. In Leslie Barker's day it was a timber building with a corrugated roof. It was rebuilt after being demolished in the 1953 floods and then again in 1978 when it was rebuilt in brick to form the new workshop. However, by 1995 Pip Reeve was ready for retiring and with no reliable and suitably skilled replacement to handle the MoT facility was closed. Brian's son Philip, who had been in the business since the age of 15 years, took over the running of the filling station and the few remaining lorries from this time, allowing Brian the opportunity to move towards semi-retirement. But by 2000 they realised the overheads were getting too high and the cut-throat competition on petrol sales, particularly from the Safeway supermarket in Fakenham, left them fighting for survival so a crucial decision was taken.

The West End Filling Station on Freeman Street, Wells With the purpose-built vehicle workshops and MoT test bay in the background – seen here in July 2000.

Seventy-nine years on from when his father and grandfather started their taxi and wood business, Brian, now himself in his early seventies, sadly closed the door and walked away from the business, the Freeman Street site being finally sold to Bugdens, the supermarket firm. Brian had hoped he would see his sons become the fourth generation of the Barkers to follow, not only in his own, but also in Herbert and Leslie's footsteps before him, and carry on in haulage to hand over the business to yet further generations in the future.

Brian and son Chris who has subsequently continued the family tradition by starting his own haulage business.

Looking back, Brian reflects on how the firm had struggled throughout the economic upheavals of dock strikes, the miner's strike, their own lorry drivers' strike, cut-throat competition, changing trading patterns, the demise of Wells as a trading port and many other obstacles. Against all these obstacles the family battled on, but stringent EU haulage legislation over recent years, draconian vehicle excise duties and ever-increasing fuel prices finally put paid to all of Brian's hopes and he was left with no alternative but to shut down the last remaining bastion of the business, the Freeman Street garage and filling station. The day of the final closure was on 13 September 2000. As he said in an interview with the *Eastern Daily Press* on 29 September 2000 under the heading 'End of the road for the great survivors':

> *"We knew we were on the way out five years ago, there's nothing new about high fuel prices. I can show you a letter I wrote to my drivers in 1994 when the price of derv went up, which could have been written yesterday. There have been an increasing number of rules and regulations, which restrict the haulier and hit the small man the hardest. The Government should have done something about it 10 years ago - it's too late for us now. The things we have done over the years, aside from haulage, have all worked for a time but there's nothing left to try. I look back to our greatest successes, which were in the 1980s when we had trade coming to us from all four sides, but when this ceased it was like operating with one arm tied behind our backs. It's very sad!"*

Footnote to the Future – The Fourth Generation

Brian's eldest son Christopher has decided to carry on the family road haulage tradition by setting up his own business, jointly with younger brother Philip and becoming the fourth generation of the family in the road haulage business. He is utilising the years of experience he gained driving for the old Barker haulage firm and using the LGV driver's licence and Certificate of Professional Competence in Road Haulage that he achieved on the way. Now with a new Operator's licence in the partnership's name, he is running a British-built ERF articulated vehicle on general haulage work.

Unusual cargo: loading a Lightning fighter jet fuselage at Narborough for Wisbech Museum.

Another jet plane, this time a Hawker Hunter destined for Brooklands Museum.

Fuel leak repairs with from the left; driver Ken Gibson, Philip Barker and driver Bob Woods.

A load of farm tractors en-route from Hull to Ben Burgess at Beeston, near Dereham, Norfolk.

Brian Barker and driver Ken Gibson with newly delivered Leyland DAF 85/400, September 1999.

The fourth generation takes over; Christopher Barker, who started his own haulage business in 2001, with his ERF EC11.

Brian in comfortable retirement, apart from providing an experienced and guiding hand to son Chris as he ventures into the haulage arena. (Picture:EDPpics)